BIG BOOK

of Bible Games

DAVID C COOK

transforming lives together

BIG BOOK OF BIBLE GAMES FOR ELEMENTARY KIDS
Published by David C Cook
4050 Lee Vance Drive
Colorado Springs, CO 80918 U.S.A.

Integrity Music Limited, a Division of David C Cook
Brighton, East Sussex BN1 2RE, England

ISBN 978-0-8307-4272-1

The content included in this book was originally published in the *Really Big Book of
Bible Games* by Gospel Light in 2006 © Gospel Light, ISBN 0-8307-4272-7.

Cover Design: James Hershberger

Printed in the United States of America
2 3 4 5 6 7 8 9 10 11

070121

Contents

How to Use This Book

If you are a teacher or a small-group leader in any children's program (Sunday school, children's worship, evening, midweek, etc.):

1. Read "Games Overview" (pp. 8–9) and "Game Leader Ideas" (p. 10) to get an understanding of the purpose and goals of *Big Book of Bible Games for Elementary Kids*.
2. Look at the contents, and then skim through this book to get an idea of the kinds of games that are provided.
3. As you prepare a lesson, use the contents and the indexes to choose games that will complement your students' understanding of the lesson. Copy game pages for your own ease of use in leading games.

If you are the children's pastor:

1. Follow the directions in numbers 1 and 2 above.
2. At the beginning of each quarter, refer to the scope and sequence of the curriculum used in your children's ministry programs. Use the contents and the indexes in this book to find games that will enrich students' understanding of the lessons. At least one week prior to a lesson, copy the needed pages and provide them to teachers and small-group leaders.
3. Consider providing a copy of *Big Book of Bible Games for Elementary Kids* for each classroom as a general resource for teachers.

Games Overview

Games are a great way for kids to have fun—and learn! *Big Book of Bible Games for Elementary Kids* is your one-stop resource for all the games you'll likely ever need for elementary kids in grades 1 through 6. Here's a quick overview of the book's three sections:

1. **Bible Learning Games**
   There are three types of games in this section. First, Bible skills games and activities help students learn basic Bible skills, such as locating Bible references, listing Bible books in order, and identifying Bible divisions. Second, Bible story review games are fun games that can be used with any Bible story. These games help children remember important facts or concepts of Bible stories. Third, Bible verse memory games also may be used with any Scripture passage. These easy-to-play games can be used anytime to help children remember life-changing Bible truths.

2. **Life Application Games**
   The second section has tons of games organized under 17 topics designed to give quick game options for Bible lessons. Scripture passages are included with each game. Also provided are discussion questions with practical tie-ins to kids' lives. Many games include options for adapting for younger or older kids, a fresh twist on a familiar game, or how to play an indoor game outside.

3. **Recreational Games**
   When you just want kids to just have fun, we have you covered! There are indoor and outdoor games, large group games, and water games. These games are great for special events or programs, camps, or any fun-filled event. Let the games begin!

Leading Games Step-by-Step:

1. **Energy-Level Indicator**
   Low: Mostly staying in seats with little movement
   Medium: Some walking or movement
   High: Lots of running, movement, and noise

2. **Location Indicator**
   In: Games that need walls, electricity, or furnishings
   Out: Games that need outdoor settings, such as water games or games that need a larger area
   In/Out: Games that could work either way; Options or Game Tips give info for making the switch from one to the other

3. **Materials**
   Common supplies are listed without the quantity needed, but unique or specific items do include the number you'll need. Optional activity materials are not listed in the materials lists.

4. **Preparation**
   This section tells you what you'll need to do before kids arrive, if anything. Preparations that take a minute or less are not included. Measuring playing areas, setting up obstacle courses, or writing on index cards are examples of preparation you may need to do. Sketches of game layouts are provided to make your game prep quick and easy.

5. **Lead the Game**
   The numbered steps allow you to lead games with ease! Bold print is used for things you can say to kids or for questions you can ask kids. Sketches show what the game looks like while playing.

6. **Options and Game Tips**
   Many games have options for adapting the game for a variety of situations. But if you don't see an option and you need one, be creative—and try your own idea! Game Tips will help you handle situations that may come up while playing games. These tips will help you become a better game leader.

7. **Discussion Questions**
   See "Leading a Good Discussion" on page 11 for tips on asking the discussion questions included with the Life Application Games in this book.

Game Leader Ideas

Creating a Playing Area
Before leading a game, give yourself plenty of time to set up the game area. You might not have much space in your classroom for a game area, so consider alternatives: outdoors, a gym, or a vacant area of the building from which sound will not carry to disturb other programs. Once you have chosen the area, plan what you will need:
- Will you need to move furniture?
- Will you need to mark boundaries? Use chalk or rope outdoors; yarn or masking tape work indoors. (Remove masking tape from carpets after games.)
- How much space will you need? Carefully review the game procedures to plan what amount and shape of space will be needed.

From time to time, take stock of your classroom area. Is it time to remove that large table or unused bookshelf? Should the chairs be rearranged or the rug put in a different place? Small changes in arrangement can result in more usable space.

Forming Groups or Teams
To keep students' interest high and to keep cliques from forming, use a variety of ways to determine teams or groups:
- Group teams by clothing color or other clothing features (wearing a sweater, wearing sneakers, etc.).
- Place equal numbers of two colors of paper squares in a bag. Kids shake the bag and draw out a square to determine teams.
- Group teams by birthday month (for two teams, January through June and July through December); adjust as needed to make numbers even.
- Group teams by the alphabetical order of kids' first or last names.
- Group teams by telling students to stand on one foot: those standing on a right foot form one team; those standing on a left foot form the other team.

After playing a round or two of a game, announce that the person on each team who is wearing the most (color), should rotate to another team. Then play the game again. As you repeat this rotation process, vary the method of rotation.

Leading the Game
Explain rules clearly and simply. It can be helpful to write the rules on the board. Make sure you explain rules step-by-step. Offer a practice round. When playing a game for the first time with your group, play it a few times just for practice. Students will learn the game's structure and rules best by actually playing the game.

Dealing with Competition
For younger kids (and for some older ones), competition can make a game uncomfortable—especially for the losers. If your group is made up primarily of younger kids, consider making a game more cooperative than competitive. You could give a special job to a child who is out, have the winning team serve a snack to the losing team, or rotate players so no one remains on the winning or losing team.

Guiding Conversation
Using guided conversation turns a game activity into discovery learning. Make use of the discussion questions provided in this book. You might ask the winning team to answer a question. You might discuss a few questions between the rounds of a game or ask questions at the beginning of the round, inviting answers when the round is over.

Leading a Good Discussion

A good discussion requires leaders to listen as much as—or more than—they speak. However, encouraging others to speak up can be difficult. The following questions are commonly asked about leading a good discussion.

How do I keep the discussion on track?
Use the discussion questions provided with the Life Application Games to focus on kids' personal experiences. When Bible truths relate to daily life, interest in the discussion will grow.

How do I get the discussion back on track?
If significant interest is shown in the new topic and it has real value, then you might decide to stay with the new issue. Otherwise, use questions to bring attention back to the original topic. Move on to a new question, restate your question, or rephrase it if students did not understand what you asked.

If an outside interruption catches the group's attention, acknowledge it as matter-of-factly as possible, and then restate the question being discussed. You may also want to summarize some of the key points already made in the discussion.

What do I do when no one says anything or when kids give "pat" answers?
If you've asked a thought-provoking question, assume that kids need at least a few moments to think. Be silent for a bit (no more than 20 to 30 seconds), then repeat or rephrase the question. If there is still no response, give an answer to the question and move on.

If silence is a recurring problem, evaluate the questions you ask. Are they too vague? Too easy? Too hard? Do they require knowledge that students don't have? Are the answers too obvious?

If the questions are fine, evaluate your response to what students say. Are you unwilling to accept answers if they differ from what you consider to be the correct responses? Do you tend to always improve the students' answers? Work to create a climate of openness and trust.

Finally, add some variety to your approach in asking questions:
- Have students write their answers on paper. This allows kids time to organize their thoughts. Then invite students to read what they wrote.
- Divide the class into smaller groups. You may ask all groups the same questions or assign different questions to each group. Invite volunteers from the groups to share the answers with everyone.

The same suggestions apply when students are giving only "pat" or simple answers.

Leading a Child to Christ

One of the greatest privileges of serving in children's ministry is to help guide children to become members of God's family. Pray and ask God to prepare the kids you know to understand and receive the good news about Jesus. Ask God to give you the sensitivity and wisdom to communicate effectively and to be aware as opportunities occur.

When talking with children about salvation, use words and phrases they understand; never assume kids understand a concept just because they can repeat certain words. Avoid symbolic terms that will confuse literal-minded thinkers. As you watch and pray, you will see kids developing relationships with God.

Here are some questions you can ask and things you can discuss with a child who is interested in accepting Jesus as their Lord and Savior. Encourage the child to look up and read the Bible verses along with you.

Read John 3:16. **Why did God send Jesus to earth?** (God loved us so much that He wants us to have eternal life with Him.)

First John 3:1 says that God wants us to be His children. But sin, doing wrong, separates us from God. Read Romans 6:23. **What do you think should happen to us when we sin?** (die) **But what is God's gift to us?** (eternal life in Jesus)

Jesus willingly died on the cross to take the punishment for our sins. Read 1 Corinthians 15:3. **But Jesus didn't stay in the tomb. After three days, He came back to life! Jesus died so that we can live forever in heaven with Him.**

Are you sorry for the wrong things that you've done? If you are, what should you do? Read 1 John 1:9. **Our sins are wiped away when we're truly sorry for what we've done and when we turn to God.**

Read Ephesians 2:8. **How are we saved?** (by God's grace, through faith) **Christian faith is a life-long adventure here on earth. With Jesus as Lord of our lives, we build a life of submitting to God, following Jesus, and keeping in step with the Spirit.**

At this point, continue to talk with the child about accepting Jesus as Lord and Savior. Include what your church teaches about how this happens. If you have any questions about salvation, talk with your pastor or children's ministry leader.

God wants *every* person to accept the free gift of eternal life that He's offering. What do *you* need to do about this?

Bible Learning Games

Bible Skills

Bible Ball Toss

Bible Skill ▶ Put Bible Books in Order

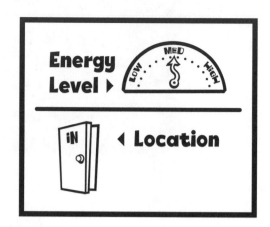

Energy Level ▶

▶ Location

Materials
Bibles, ball

Preparation
Make copies of the contents page from a Bible
(1 per student).

Lead the Game
1. **It's easier to find places in the Bible when we know the order of the books. Let's practice saying the books of the Bible in order.**
2. Distribute copies of the Bible contents page for students to review.
3. Have kids stand in a circle. Toss a ball to a student and say, "Genesis." The student who catches the ball says, "Exodus," then tosses the ball to another student. Continue tossing the ball and saying the names of the books of the Bible in order until all the books have been named. Keep playing the game as time permits.

Options
1. For younger kids, limit the number of books named, gradually adding more books as students are able to recall them.
2. For older students, form more than one circle, and have circles compete to see which circle of kids can say the names of Bible books in a specific division of the Bible, such as the Minor Prophets.

Game Tip
If some kids are unfamiliar with the books of the Bible, ask students to take turns reading aloud the names, referring to the Bible contents page. As students say the names, print the Bible book names in order on a large sheet of paper. Display the paper where all students can see it.

Big Book of Bible Games
for Elementary Kids
© David C Cook. Permission granted to photocopy for ministry purposes only.

Book Guess

Bible Skill ▶ Identify and Spell Books

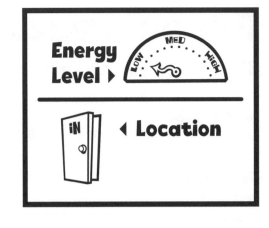

Materials
Bibles, whiteboard and dry-erase marker
(or large sheet of paper and marker)

Lead the Game
1. Lead students to play a game similar to Hangman. On the board or a large sheet of paper, draw blank lines for each letter of a Bible book.
2. Students are to guess letters of the alphabet. Print correct letters on the appropriate blank lines. Print incorrect letters to the side of the blank lines, and print one letter of the word *Bible*. Kids try to guess and find the correct book in their Bibles before the word *Bible* is completed. The student who correctly guesses the word secretly chooses a different book of the Bible and draws lines for other kids to guess. Continue playing the game as time permits.

Game Tip
If playing this game with only a specific section of the Bible, introduce the game by making a comment such as: **Today we're going to play a game to find out more about the second group of books in the Old Testament part of the Bible. These books are called the books of History because they tell the history of how God brought Abraham's descendants back to their homeland many years after Abraham died. These books also tell about how the people obeyed God and disobeyed Him.** Referring to the contents page in their Bibles, kids can take turns reading aloud the names of the books of History: Joshua, Judges, Ruth, 1 Samuel, 2 Samuel, 1 Kings, 2 Kings, 1 Chronicles, 2 Chronicles, Ezra, Nehemiah, Esther. Students could also find each book in their Bibles.

Gospel Puzzles

Bible Skill ▸ Locate References: New Testament

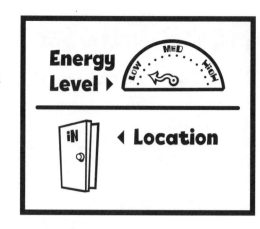

Energy Level ▸

iN ◂ Location

Materials
Bibles; index cards; blue, red, purple, and green markers; scissors

Preparation
Print, in the colors indicated, the following references on separate index cards: blue—Matthew 21:1–3; Mark 11:1–3; Luke 19:28–31; red—Mark 11:4–6; Luke 19:32–34; purple—Matthew 21:9; Mark 11:9–10; Luke 19:38; John 12:13; green—Matthew 21:15–16; Mark 11:18; Luke 19:39–40. Cut each card into two puzzle pieces as shown in the sketch.

Lead the Game
1. Count the number of students present. Ask kids to close their eyes while you hide puzzle pieces, making sure to hide one piece for each student. Use all the cards of one color before using another color. You can participate in this activity if you have an uneven number of players. Each student should find a hidden puzzle piece and then find the student holding the matching puzzle piece. Kids can then turn to the Bible verses.
2. Invite kids to read their Bible verses aloud. **In what section of the Bible are these verses found?** (the Gospels) **What is similar about all the (blue) passages?** (They tell what Jesus told His disciples to do.) **How are the (blue) passages different from each other? Each gospel tells the story of Jesus' life in a slightly different way. The people who wrote these books included different information about the same events. When we read the different accounts of each event, we get a better idea of everything that happened.**
3. Repeat the activity as time permits, hiding different puzzle pieces or hiding the same pieces again.

Mark 11:4-6

Mixed-Up Books

Bible Skill ▸ Identify Bible Divisions:
New Testament

Energy
Level ▸

◂ Location

Materials
Bibles, index cards, marker, masking tape

Preparation
Print the names of the books of the New Testament on index cards,
one name per card. On separate cards, print the names of the main
divisions of New Testament books (Gospels, History, Letters, Prophecy). Make at least two sets of cards or one set
of book and main division cards for every ten students. Tear masking tape into 3" strips, making at least 56 strips
of tape. Place strips on a table or chair where they can be easily removed by kids.

Lead the Game
1. Mix up the book cards you prepared. One at a time, hold up the cards. Students are to tell
   which division each book is part of. **All the stories in the Bible—from Adam and Eve
   to the very
   end—fit
   together
   to show
   us God's
   great plan for**

   **the world and for our own lives. In the New Testament part of the Bible, we read about the coming of the
   Savior whom God promised to send. We also read about all the great things that happened after God kept
   His promise.**
2. Divide the class into at least two teams of no more than ten students each. Teams are to line up in single-file
   lines at the opposite side of the classroom from where the masking-tape strips are. Place a set of mixed-up
   book cards facedown in a pile on the floor next to the first student on each team. Tape a set of main division
   cards on the wall across from each team, near the masking-tape strips. Leave room under each division card
   for book cards to be taped.
3. At your signal, the first student in each line takes a book card, runs to the division cards, grabs a piece of tape,
   and tapes the book card to the wall below the correct division card. Students then return to their teams and tag
   the next students in line. Play continues until all the cards are on the wall under the correct category.

Game Tip
If your students are not familiar with the New Testament divisions, go over this before playing the game.

People Scrabble

Bible Skill ▶ Locate References: New Testament

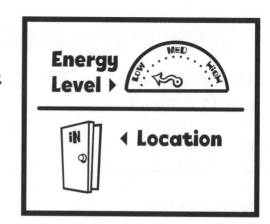

Energy Level ▶

iN   ◀ Location

Materials
Bibles, graph paper, pencils, index cards

Preparation
On a sheet of graph paper, outline a grid with at least 20 vertical and horizontal columns. On separate index cards, print these Bible references: Matthew 1:18; 2:1; 2:13; Luke 1:5, 19, 26–27; 2:1, 8, 10, 46.

Lead the Game
1. **What do you think are some of the most famous stories in the Bible? Accept responses.** (creation, Noah's ark, David and Goliath, Jesus' miracles) **Why are these stories so famous?** (The stories are exciting! They tell about important things.) **Some stories in the Bible are so important that they are written about more than once. The events that happened during the time when Jesus was born and grew as a child are described in several different books of the Bible. What are the books called which tell about Jesus' life?** (the Gospels: Matthew, Mark, Luke, and John) **Let's practice finding Scriptures in these books.**

2. Group students into small groups. Place index cards facedown near the grid you've prepared. At your signal, each group chooses an index card and finds the Bible reference(s) printed on the card. Kids in each group

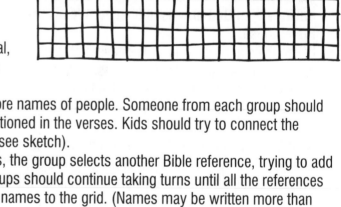

should find and read the verses to discover one or more names of people. Someone from each group should print on the graph paper the names of the people mentioned in the verses. Kids should try to connect the names together as in a Scrabble® crossword game (see sketch).

3. If a group is unable to connect a name to other names, the group selects another Bible reference, trying to add the first name(s) to the grid later in the game. The groups should continue taking turns until all the references have been read or until there is no more space to add names to the grid. (Names may be written more than once.) **What are some of the events these names remind you of? What are some things you know about these people? Accept responses.**

Game Tip
If you don't have graph paper, draw a grid on a large sheet of paper.

Big Book of Bible Games
for Elementary Kids
© David C Cook. Permission granted to photocopy for ministry purposes only.

Promise Search

Bible Skill ▸ Locate References: Old Testament

Energy Level ▸

iN ◂ **Location**

Materials
Bibles, whiteboard and dry-erase marker (or large sheet of paper and markers)

Preparation
Print these Bible references on the board in random order, leaving room to write near each reference: Genesis 8:22; Exodus 15:13; 20:12; Deuteronomy 4:29; Joshua 1:9; 1 Samuel 26:23; 2 Chronicles 7:14; Nehemiah 9:31.

Lead the Game
1. **God's promises are written about in the Bible.** Draw students' attention to the board. **Each of these Bible verses tells about a promise God made or something that we can depend on God to do. These verses are all in the first two divisions of the Bible. What are these divisions called?** (Law and History)
2. Group students into small groups. Assign each group a Bible reference. The students in each group should read their assigned verse and choose a key word about the promise. To help groups choose key words, ask: **Which word is the most important in this verse? Why? Which word helps you understand the main idea of the verse?**

Joshua 1:9

3. Have a volunteer from one of the groups say a word that rhymes with their key word. Other students try to guess the key word. The volunteer says rhyming words until the key word is guessed correctly. Ask a volunteer from the group to read the Bible verse. Have another volunteer write on the board the key word near the Scripture reference.

Game Tips
Have kids turn to the contents page in their Bibles. Ask them to say with you the books of Law and History (Genesis through Esther). You can also suggest to students that they can refer to the contents page in their Bibles when they need help locating a specific Bible book.

Prophet Talk

Bible Skill ▸ Identify Bible Divisions:
Old Testament—Prophecy

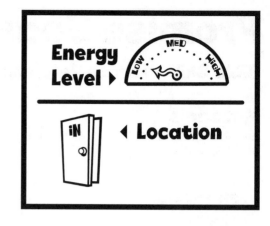

Energy
Level ▸

iN ◂ Location

Materials
Bibles, whiteboard, dry-erase marker and eraser
(or large sheet of paper and marker), children's music from
your collection, music player

Preparation
Print on the board or on a sheet of paper the books of the Major and
Minor Prophets in order.

Lead the Game
1. Have kids sit on the floor in a circle. Ask a volunteer to
   read from the board the names of the Bible books. **God
   sent many messengers, called prophets, to His people.
   These prophets spoke or wrote what God wanted His
   people to know. They gave many warnings to obey
   God and many promises about the Savior who was
   coming. We can read these messages in the books
   of Prophecy. The first five books of prophecy are
   called the Major Prophets, because these books
   are longer than the Minor Prophets. The Minor
   Prophets are the 12 smaller books that complete
   the Old Testament.**
2. Tell kids to play a game of Hot Potato, passing the
   eraser or a marker while the music plays. When the
   music stops, say either "Major Prophets" or "Minor
   Prophets." The student with the eraser erases a Bible book name
   from the division you named. If using paper and markers, the
   student crosses out the name.
3. Continue playing until all the books are erased or crossed out. Ask
   students to repeat together the names of the books of the Major and Minor Prophets.

Game Tips
1. If you have a student who is reluctant to play the game, let that student start and stop the music.
2. Sit in the circle with the students. Students enjoy getting to know their teachers while playing games together!

Walk and Talk

Bible Skill ▸ Identify Bible Divisions:
New Testament

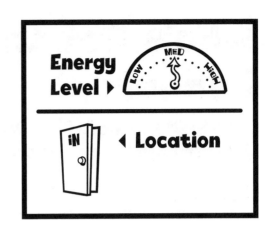

Energy Level ▸

◂ Location

Materials
Bibles, roll paper, tape, markers, children's music from your collection, music player

Preparation
Cover a table with roll paper. Draw lines to divide the paper into sections, one section per student. Print the names of the divisions of the New Testament in separate sections, repeating divisions as needed ("Gospels," "History," "Letters," "Prophecy").

Lead the Game
1. **The New Testament tells how God's promise to send a Savior came true and how God's keeping of His promise brought salvation to all people!**

2. While you play music, tell kids to hold their Bibles as they walk around the table. When you stop the music, each student should put a hand on one section on the paper. Then each kid should refer to the contents page in a Bible to find a book in the New Testament from that division. When students are ready, each can say the division and book name aloud. Repeat as time permits.

3. Turn the roll paper over and tape it to the table. Students should walk around the table while you play music. When you stop the music, call out a New Testament division. Each student should write the name of a book in that division. Play several rounds of the game.

Game Tips
1. Introduce the New Testament divisions by saying: **The word *gospel* means "good news." The four gospels tell the good news about Jesus. The History book, Acts, tells what God's Holy Spirit did through people who told the good news about Jesus to the rest of the world. The next division of the New Testament is Letters. The Letters were written to encourage people to live as Christians. The last division is Prophecy. Revelation, the only book of prophecy, tells about the future time when Jesus will come back to earth.**
2. You could give each student a copy of a Bible contents page to use in playing the game.

Who's Got the Beans?

Bible Skill ▸ Identify Bible Divisions:
Old Testament—Law, History, Poetry

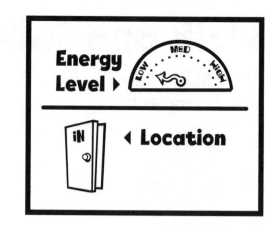

Energy Level ▸

iN ◂ Location

Materials
Bibles, 10 beans per student (or other small objects for each student), children's music from your collection, music player

Lead the Game
1. Ask students to open their Bibles to the contents page. **Which books are in the Law division of the Old Testament?** (Genesis through Deuteronomy) Ask volunteers to read the names of the books of Law aloud. Identify the books of History and Poetry in the same way.
2. Give each student ten beans. Group students into two equal teams: A and B. (You can participate if you have an uneven number of kids.) As you play music, students should move randomly around the room. When you stop the music, each student should find a partner from the other team. Call out either A or B. Each student in the named group is to say the name of a book in one of the first three divisions of the Old Testament (Law, History, Poetry). The kids' partners should respond by saying the name of the correct division and then naming another book in the division. (Optional: If students are unfamiliar with Bible book names, let them use the contents page in their Bibles to find book names.) If the division named is correct, the first student gives his or her partner a bean. If the division named is incorrect, the partner gives the first student a bean. Keep playing as time permits. The object of the game is to have the most beans at the end of the playing period.

Game Tips
1. Coins or uncooked pasta shapes can be used instead of beans.
2. Before playing, briefly review the first three divisions of the Old Testament: **The books of Law tell about the beginning of the world and record God's instructions to His people. The books of History tell how God led His people to a new land and give us stories about their leaders. The books of Poetry are stories, songs, sayings, and poems about how great and wonderful God is and how we can live in ways that please Him.**

Bible Learning Games

Bible Story Review

Chair Scramble

Bible Skill ▸ Bible Story Review

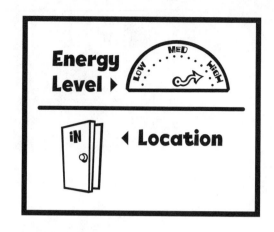

Materials
Bibles, paper, markers, 4 large index cards, tape, 4 chairs

Preparation
Choose a Bible story students have studied. On a sheet of paper, list true or false statements about events in the Bible story. Letter one index card "True" and another index card "False." Tape the labeled index cards to chairs (sketch a).

Lead the Game
1. Divide the class into two equal teams. (If you have an extra student, he or she could read aloud the true or false statements.) Have the teams sit on the floor as shown in sketch b. Assign each child a number.
2. After teams are seated, read aloud a statement about the Bible story, and then call out a number. The students from each team with that number jump up and run to sit in their team's "True" or "False" chair. The student who sits in the correct chair first scores a point for his or her team. In case of a tie, each team scores a point. Repeat the process until all true or false statements have been read. For false statements, pause and ask students to correct them.
3. Keep playing as time permits. Ask: **What did you learn from this Bible story? What are the most interesting things about this Bible story? What are the most surprising things about this Bible story?**

a.

b.

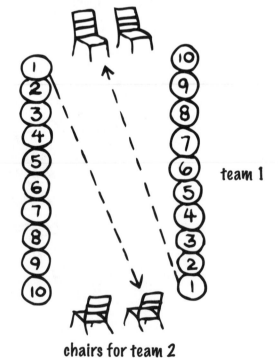

Chopstick Relay

Bible Skill ▸ Bible Story Review

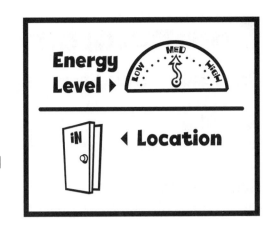

Materials
Bibles, paper, marker, 2 large bowls, 3 Asian-style takeout food containers, marker, whiteboard and dry-erase marker (or roll paper and marker), Ping-Pong balls (or large marshmallows, 1 per student), set of chopsticks (1 per student)

Preparation
Choose a Bible story that kids are familiar with. On a sheet of paper, list true and false statements about events in the Bible story, and list events not in the story. Example: Ruth was Naomi's daughter-in-law. (true) Ruth and Naomi moved to Egypt. (false) Naomi loved to sew. (not in story). Label one takeout container "True," one "False," and one "Not in Story" (sketch a). Place the same number of Ping-Pong balls or marshmallows in each bowl. Place the containers on a table on one side of the room, and place the bowls on the floor on the opposite side of the room.

Lead the Game
1. Divide the class into two equal teams. (If you have an extra student, he or she may read aloud the true or false statements and keep score.) Teams line up between bowls and containers as shown in sketch b. Give each player a set of chopsticks.

2. Read aloud a statement about the Bible story and say "Go." The first player in line uses chopsticks to pick up a ball or marshmallow. Using the chopsticks, the player passes the ball or marshmallow to the next player. The ball or marshmallow is passed most easily if it rests on top of the chopsticks (sketch c). Play continues until the ball or marshmallow reaches the end of the line. Using the chopsticks, the last player carries the ball or marshmallow and drops it into the correct food container. The player then goes to the front of the line. The first student to put the ball or marshmallow into the correct container scores a point for his or her team. In case of a tie, each team scores a point.

3. Keep playing until all players have had a turn. Ask: **What part of this Bible story is the most interesting? Surprising? Why? What did you learn from this Bible story?**

a. TRUE FALSE NOT IN STORY

b.

c.

Community Chaos

Bible Skill ▸ Bible Story Review

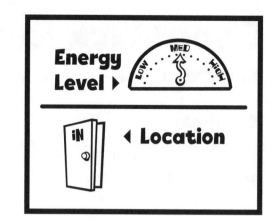

Materials
Bibles, 20 large index cards, marker

Preparation
Choose a Bible story or Bible memory verse students have studied. List ten events from the story (or words from the verse), one event (or word) on each card (sketch a). Make two identical sets of cards.

Lead the Game

1. Divide the class into two teams. Teams line up as in sketch b. Shuffle both sets of cards together; then spread all cards facedown on the floor between the teams.
2. Assign each student on one team a community occupation (bus driver, firefighter, police officer, librarian, doctor, barber, teacher, hairstylist, baker, crossing guard, etc.). Assign players on the other team the same occupations. To begin play, call out a job description such as, "I drive people from one place to another." Each of the two kids who have that occupation quickly chooses any card on the floor and takes it back to his or her team. Repeat the process by calling out another job description. As kids take cards to their teams, team members try to place their cards in the correct story sequence or word order. If a student takes a duplicate card, the player who is called next returns that card to the pile before choosing a new card. The team that first places all the cards in the correct order wins.
3. Discuss the Bible story by asking questions such as: **Which of these events was the most important? Why? What did the people in the Bible story do? What did you learn from this Scripture passage?**

a.

Jesus visited Mary and Martha.	Martha cleaned the house.	Mary talked to Jesus.
Martha became angry.	Jesus loves both Mary and Martha.	Jesus was arrested and crucified.
Mary and Martha were sad and cried.	Jesus rose from the dead.	Jesus died so we could be forgiven.

Each person has a special place in God's family.

b.

Big Book of Bible Games
for Elementary Kids
© David C Cook. Permission granted to photocopy for ministry purposes only.

Count Your Cards!

Bible Skill ▶ Bible Story Review

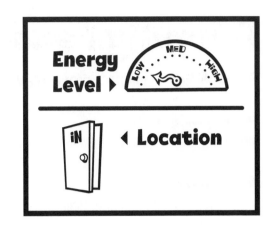

Energy Level ▶

iN ◀ Location

Materials
Bibles, 30 large index cards, pen, number cube

Preparation
On each index card, print a true or false statement about one or more Bible stories kids have studied. Or type the statements and cut them apart.

Lead the Game
1. Place cards facedown in six columns with five cards to a column. Divide the class into two teams. A player from the first team rolls the number cube. Whatever the number on the top of the cube is, the player should count that many spaces from the top left card across the row to the right. The player turns over the card (see sketch) and reads the statement aloud.
2. The player's team should work together to identify the statement as either true or false. If a correct response is given, the team keeps the card. If an incorrect response is given, the player replaces the card facedown. If the statement is false, the team must correct the statement in order to gain the card. A player from the second team repeats the process, counting from the card that was turned over. Play continues in this manner. When all the cards have been collected or time is up, the team with the most cards wins the game.

Luke preached to the crowd on Pentecost

Friendly Feud

Bible Skill ▶ Bible Story Review

Energy Level ▶

◀ Location

Materials
Bibles, paper, call bell, whiteboard, dry-erase marker

Preparation
Print or type questions about Bible stories students have studied.

Lead the Game
1. Divide the class into two teams. Have teams sit in chairs facing each other. Place the call bell on a table between the two teams.
2. The first player from each team goes to the table and stands with one hand on the table and one hand behind his or her back. Read aloud the first question. The first person to ring the bell may answer the question. If the answer is correct, that team gets ten points. If the answer is incorrect, the other player may give an answer, winning five points for his or her team. If neither player gives the correct answer, you can ask the question again later in the game. Keep playing until all students have had several turns. Keep score on the board.
3. When the game is over, ask: **What is the most important thing to remember from this Bible story? Why? What is something surprising that happened in this Bible story?**

Fruit Pop

Bible Skill ▸ Bible Story Review

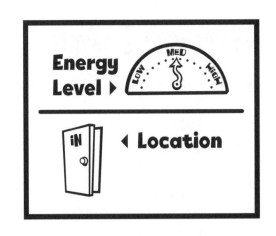
Materials
Bibles, strips of paper, pen, balloons in a variety of colors, large plastic bags

Preparation
Choose a Bible story students have studied. List ten events from the story, one event on each strip of paper (see sketch). Roll the paper strips and insert each one into a balloon. Inflate the balloons and tie. Put balloons into a large plastic bag. Make an identical set of balloons for each team of six to eight students. (Optional: Make one set of all orange balloons and label the bag "oranges." Make another set of purple balloons and label the bag "grapes," and so forth.)

Lead the Game
1. Divide the class into teams of six to eight students. Give each team a plastic bag with balloons. At your signal, students should remove the balloons from the bag, pop them, and put the Bible story events in the correct sequence. (If a student doesn't like the noise of balloons popping, allow him or her the choice of watching the fun or helping with the sequencing.)
2. After the teams have put their strips in order, discuss the Bible story by asking questions, such as: **Which of these events was the most important? Why? What do you learn about God from this story? Which character showed (patience)? How?**

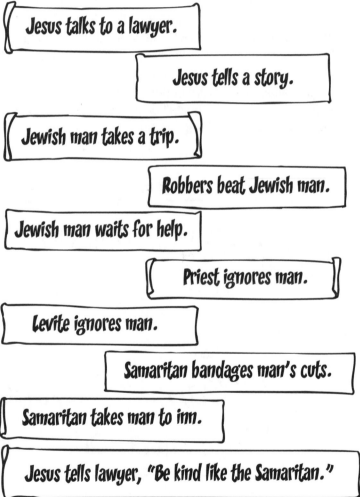

Jesus talks to a lawyer.

Jesus tells a story.

Jewish man takes a trip.

Robbers beat Jewish man.

Jewish man waits for help.

Priest ignores man.

Levite ignores man.

Samaritan bandages man's cuts.

Samaritan takes man to inn.

Jesus tells lawyer, "Be kind like the Samaritan."

Hit or Miss

Bible Skill ▶ Bible Story Review

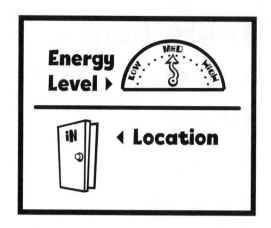

Energy Level ▶

◀ Location

Materials

Bibles, large piece of paper, marker, masking tape, blindfold

Preparation

Print on the paper 10 to 15 words that were mentioned in a Bible story students have recently studied. Then add some words that don't have anything to do with the story (see sketch). Attach the paper to a wall at the students' eye level.

Lead the Game

1. Blindfold a volunteer. At a distance of about 5' from the paper on the wall, turn the volunteer around three times, and direct him or her toward the paper. The volunteer is to touch the paper with an index finger. Remove the blindfold. If the volunteer "hit" a word by touching it, he or she should tell if the word is a part of the Bible story. If the word belongs, the volunteer (or classmate chosen by the volunteer) is to use the word in a sentence telling information from the Bible story. If the volunteer "missed" touching a word, blindfold the student again and let him or her try to "hit" a word again.
2. Repeat the process with additional volunteers until all the words have been used. Ask: **What is an important thing to remember about this Bible story? Why?**

Cornelius   prison   dream   dinner

tree   Joppa   Caesarea   animals

Gentile   soldiers

unclean   bread   sheet   Peter

angel   salvation   robbers   Jewish

Big Book of Bible Games
for Elementary Kids

Question Cube

Bible Skill ▶ Bible Story Review

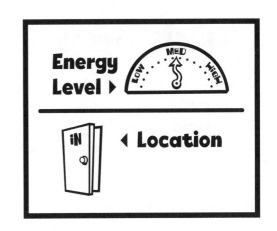

Energy Level ▶ LOW MED HIGH

iN ◀ Location

Materials

Bibles, square box (6" x 6" or larger), marker, whiteboard, dry-erase marker (Optional: roll paper, scissors, tape)

Preparation

If necessary, cover the box with roll paper. On the sides of the box, print a different word or phrase on each side: *Who*, *What*, *When*, *Where*, *Why*, *Free points!*

Lead the Game

1. Divide the class into two teams. The play begins as a volunteer from Team A rolls the question cube. If the word *Why* lands face up, the volunteer must use the word in a question about the story. For example, in the parable of the lost son, a question might be: "Why did the son want to leave his father's home?"
2. Players on Team B who want to answer the question must stand up. The first player who stands gets to answer the question. Continue the game, alternating letting the teams roll the cube. For each correct answer, a team is given ten points. Keep score on the board. When the game is over, say: **You remembered a lot of facts from our Bible story! What did you learn about God? What did you learn about how God wants you to live?**

Game Tip

For younger students, or if you think your students will have difficulty coming up with questions, you may want to have a list of questions prepared that can be read by the students.

Quick Draw

Bible Skill ▸ Bible Story Review

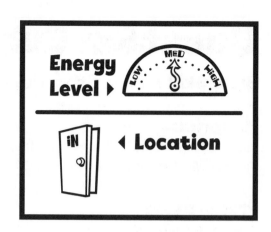

Energy Level ▸

◀ Location

Materials

Bibles, slips of paper, pen, box, whiteboard, dry-erase marker (or roll paper taped to the wall, markers)

Preparation

On separate slips of paper, print ten or more words or phrases mentioned in a Bible story that students have recently studied. (Example: *Jesus*, *expert in the law*, *robbers*, *clothes*, *road*, *priest*, *Levite*, *donkey*, *wounds*, *Samaritan*, *inn*)

Lead the Game

1. Divide the class into two teams, and have each team sit on the floor as far away from each other as possible. Each team is to choose one artist and one runner. Place a chair between the teams (see sketch). You can stand near the whiteboard or paper. At your signal, the artist from each team walks quickly to you, reads the word or phrase on a slip of paper you are holding, and returns to his or her team. Artists quickly draw a picture of the word or phrase without speaking or drawing letters or words. The teams try to guess the correct word or phrase. When a team has the correct answer, the team runner walks quickly to the chair, sits in it, and calls out word or phrase. Award that team ten points.

2. Have the teams choose a different artist and runner for each round. When all the words have been drawn, the team with the most points wins. At the end of the game, ask questions such as: **What did you learn about God from this story? Which character showed (kindness)? How? How can you show kindness?**

Game Tip

For younger students, whisper words or phrases instead of writing them on slips of paper.

Sentence Connect

Bible Skill ▸ Bible Story Review

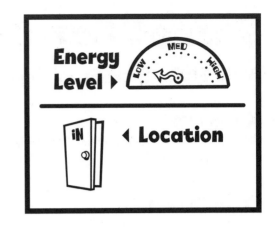

Energy Level ▸ LOW MED HIGH

iN ◂ Location

Materials
Bibles, poster board, scissors, marker

Preparation
To make game cards, cut poster board into sixteen 4" squares. Use a marker to number the cards 1 through 16. On the opposite side of the cards, print eight sentences from a Bible story students have recently studied—half a sentence on each card (see sketch). Make one set of game cards for each small group of kids.

Lead the Game
1. Place the cards, numbered sides up, on the floor or a table. Have kids take turns turning over two cards at a time. If the two cards chosen make a complete sentence, the student may keep the cards and take another turn.
2. When all the cards have been matched, ask kids to read the sentences in the correct order. Ask: **What is something new you learned from this Bible story? What did you learn about Jesus?**

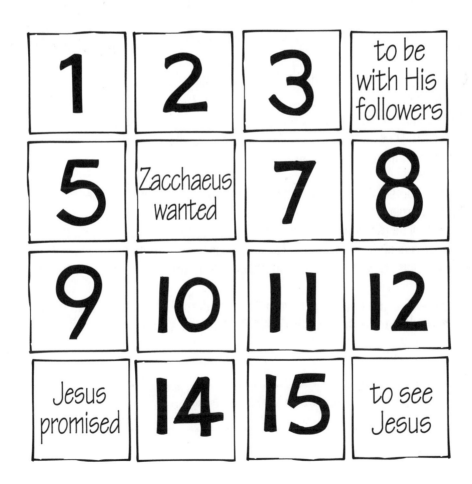

Street Corners

Bible Skill ▶ Bible Story Review

Materials
Bibles, scissors, poster board, marker, masking tape, red and green construction paper, 2 rulers, paper, whiteboard, dry-erase marker

Preparation
To make street signs, cut and label poster board as shown in sketch a. Tape street signs in four different corners of your room. Cut red and green construction paper into matching octagon shapes. Print "Stop" on red paper and "Go" on green paper. Tape a ruler onto each octagon shape (sketch b). On a sheet of paper, list several what, where, why, and who questions about the session's Bible story (sketch c). Make an equal number of each type of question.

a.
WHAT ST.
WHERE AVE.
WHY RD.
WHO DR.

c.
What did Jonathan and David do when they said good-bye?
Where did David hide from Saul?
Who did David marry?
Why did Saul want to kill David?

Lead the Game
1. Divide the class into four teams. Stand in the center of the room and hold up the Go sign while teams walk around the perimeter of the room. After several seconds, hold up the Stop sign. Teams should walk quickly to the nearest corner and sit down. (Each team must be in a different corner.)
2. The first team to have all its members seated at the same corner receives five points. Once all the teams are seated, the teacher asks each team a question that corresponds with its street sign. When a team answers correctly, it gets five points. Keep track of the points on the board. Play resumes when the Go sign is held up again.
3. The game continues until all the questions have been answered. The team with the most points wins. Ask: **What do you learn about God from this story? What surprised you about this Bible story?**

Big Book of Bible Games for Elementary Kids

That's the Way It Was

Bible Skill ▸ Bible Story Review

Energy Level ▸ LOW MED HIGH

iN ◂ Location

Materials
Bibles, slips of paper, pen

Preparation
Prepare a slip of paper for each child, minus one. Print on each slip of paper a word that is repeated several times in a Bible story. Place chairs in a circle.

Lead the Game
1. Ask kids to sit on chairs. Choose a volunteer to stand in the middle. Give one slip of paper to each student who is seated. Read or tell a Bible story with expression. Each time you say a word that is on a slip of paper, the student holding that paper must stand, turn around, and sit down again in the same chair. Meanwhile, the player in the middle tries to sit on the same chair. If the player in the middle succeeds, the student now without a seat becomes the player in the middle and gives his or her slip of paper to the student now seated.
2. Continue telling the story at a pace that is comfortable for your students.
    Ask: **How can what you've learned from this Bible story help you to better follow Jesus?**

Option
For an added challenge, insert the phrase "That's the way it was!" at various times during the story. Whenever you say this phrase, all kids must stand and find a new seat. The player in the middle can use this opportunity to find a seat. As you continue with the story, the student left without a seat will be the player in the middle.

Toss 'n Tell

Bible Skill ▸ Bible Story Review

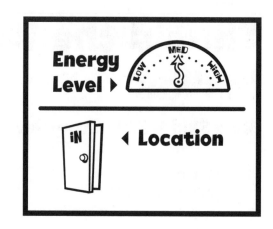

Energy Level ▸

◂ **Location**

Materials
Bibles, long length of roll paper, marker, tape measure, beanbag

Preparation
Divide the paper into nine sections. Label the sections as follows: Who? What? When? Where? Why? Put four Xs on the paper as shown in the sketch.

Lead the Game
1. Place the paper on the floor in an open area of your room. Have kids stand at least four feet from the paper. Each student takes a turn tossing the beanbag onto the paper. Kids then review the Bible story by answering the type of question on which the beanbag landed. (Example: Who? Abraham and Sarah. What? God promised Abraham a child. When? In Old Testament times. Where? In the promised land of Canaan. Why? Because God wanted to make a great nation out of Abraham's descendants.)
2. When the beanbag lands on an X, the student keeps tossing the beanbag until it lands on a question. When the game is finished, ask: **What is the most important thing you've learned about God from this story? What surprised you about this Bible story?**

Big Book of Bible Games
for Elementary Kids
© David C Cook. Permission granted to photocopy for ministry purposes only.

We Got It!

Bible Skill ▶ Bible Story Review

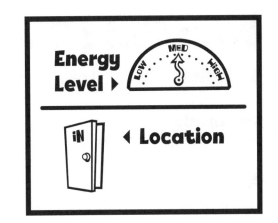

Energy Level ▶

iN ◀ **Location**

Materials
Bibles, large index cards, marker, whiteboard, dry-erase marker

Preparation
Print the letters of the alphabet on index cards—one letter per card. Omit the letters Q and X. Make two sets of alphabet cards.

Lead the Game
1. Divide the group into two teams. Give each team a set of alphabet cards. Help the teams to divide the cards as evenly as possible among team members. Then call out a word or name from a Bible story that students have studied. The players with those letters must arrange themselves to correctly spell the word. (A player who is holding two or more letters used in the word must reach around other players to hold those letters in the correct order. A player who is holding a letter which is used more than once should stand at the first position where the letter occurs.)

2. As soon as a team has the letters in the correct order, members of the team are to shout, "We got it!" The other team must then freeze in position. Ask the players on the first team who are not holding letters to spell the word aloud. The players who are holding letters used more than once must run to the next position(s) where the letter appears as the word is spelled aloud. Correct spelling is worth ten points, but an error deducts five points. Then the other team can attempt to correctly spell the word.

3. When a word has been spelled correctly, have a player tell its meaning or explain how the word is used in the Bible story. When finished with the game, ask: **How can knowing this story help you love Jesus more? What did you learn about Jesus from this Bible story?**

Game Tip
Play a practice round before you begin keeping score.

Who Said That?

Bible Skill ▸ Bible Story Review

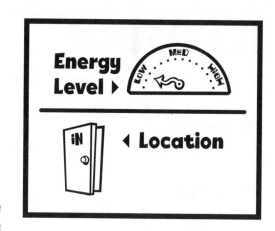

Materials

Bibles, digital voice recorder, whiteboard, dry-erase marker

Preparation

Record various phrases that were spoken by characters in one or more Bible stories that students have studied. You could use a different voice for each phrase!

Lead the Game

1. Divide the group into two teams, and ask students to sit. Play the first recorded phrase. Then ask, **"Who said that?"** Call on the first student who stands to answer the question. If the answer is correct, that team gets ten points. If the answer is incorrect, let someone from the other team answer. Then ask, **"Why did he (or she) say that?"** Call on the first person who stands to answer the question. If the answer is incorrect, let someone from the other team answer.

2. Continue until all the phrases have been identified. Ask: **What did you learn that can help you please God more?**

Bible Learning Games

Bible Verse Memory

Around the Verse

Bible Skill ▶ Bible Verse Memory

Energy Level ▶ LOW MED HIGH

iN ◀ **Location**

Materials
Bible; long length of roll paper; marker; small, unbreakable object; children's music from your collection; music player; individually wrapped candy

Preparation
Print the words of a Bible memory verse on a large length of paper, dividing the verse into seven or eight phrases.

Lead the Game
1. Have students sit in a circle around the paper you prepared. As you play music, tell students to pass the object around the circle. When the music stops, the student holding the object says the first phrase of the verse (see sketch). The student on his or her right says the next phrase of the verse.
2. Continue around the circle until the entire verse has been quoted. The last student places a piece of candy on a word on the paper. Repeat the activity until all the words are covered or as time permits.
3. Then let students enjoy some candy! Discuss the verse while kids are eating. Ask: **What does this verse mean? What do you learn from this verse?**

Game Tip
If you have students who cannot eat candy, be sure to provide other snacks such as crackers or raisins.

Balloon Bop

Bible Skill ▸ Bible Verse Memory

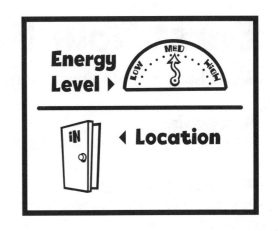
Materials
Bibles, balloons, masking tape, long length of roll paper, permanent markers

Preparation
Blow up and tie balloons (one for each pair of students). In an open area, use masking tape to make a long line on the floor. Print a Bible memory verse on the paper, and hang it on a wall for reference.

Lead the Game
Divide the class into pairs. Have pairs of students stand on opposite sides of the line. Give one kid in each pair an inflated balloon. Pairs of students tap the balloon back and forth across the line to each other, repeating the words of the Bible memory verse in order.

Options
1. Have students stand in a circle and tap the balloon around the circle, repeating the words of the Bible memory verse in order.
2. Instead of tapping balloons back and forth, students in each pair sit on opposite sides of a table and slide coins across the table to each other. Ask: **What questions do you have about this verse? What in this verse do you need to share with someone?**

Burst Your Bubble

Bible Skill ▶ Bible Verse Memory

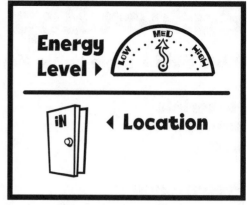

Energy Level ▶

◀ **Location**

Materials
Bibles, slips of paper, marker, balloons, garbage bag

Preparation
Print one to three words of a Bible memory verse on separate slips of paper, making one paper for each student. (Repeat key words of a verse as needed.) Blow up the balloons and insert one rolled slip of paper into each balloon before tying. Put balloons in a garbage bag to transport them to class.

Lead the Game
1. Have each student choose a balloon, pop it, and find the paper inside.
2. Tell kids to read the verse in their Bibles and arrange the slips of paper in memory verse order. Ask: **How will following the truths of this verse help you love God more?**

Fill-in-the-Blanks

Bible Skill ▸ Bible Verse Memory

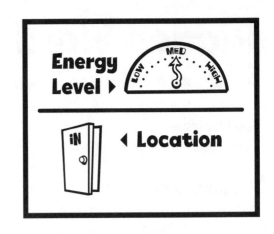

Energy Level ▸

Location ▸ in

Materials
Bibles, index cards, marker, pencils, lined paper

Preparation
Print each word of a Bible memory verse on a separate index card. Number the cards in verse order, writing numbers on the backs of the cards.

Lead the Game
1. Give each student a sheet of lined paper and a pencil. Tell students the number of words in the Bible memory verse. Students should number the lines on their paper for the same number of words. Distribute the prepared index cards. Depending on the number of students in your group, some kids may have more than one card.
2. Tell students to move around the room. They should ask other kids what numbers and words are on their cards and write the words on the corresponding numbered lines on their papers. When finished, students can read the verse together. Ask: **What is the most important part of this verse to you?**

Hidden Words

Bible Skill ▶ Bible Verse Memory

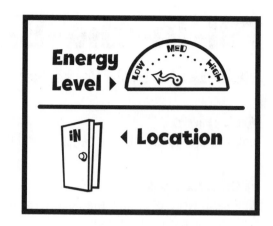

Energy Level ▶ LOW MED HIGH

iN ◀ Location

Materials
Bibles, index cards in a variety of colors, marker, scissors

Preparation
Print the words of a Bible memory verse on same-colored index cards, one word per card. Cut the cards in half. Hide the cut-up cards in the room. Make a set of cards for each small group of students, each set in a different color.

Lead the Game
1. Divide the class into as many groups as the number of card sets you made. Invite the groups to search for the cards. Once a student in a group finds the first card, his or her group keeps looking for the rest of the same-colored cards.
2. Students should put their cards together to find the words of the Bible memory verse. Students should then find the verse in their Bibles and put the cards in order. Ask all the kids to read the verse aloud. Ask: **What does this verse teach us about God?**

Big Book of Bible Games for Elementary Kids

Listen Up!

Bible Skill ▸ Bible Verse Memory

Energy Level ▸

LOW MED HIGH

iN ◂ Location

Materials
Bible, 2 sheets of paper, marker, blindfold

Preparation
Divide the words of a Bible memory verse into two parts. Print each part on a separate sheet of paper.

Lead the Game

1. Play a game similar to Marco Polo. Ask a volunteer to stand on one side of the room, and blindfold that volunteer. The rest of the students should stand on the other side of room. Give the papers you prepared to two students who then quietly position themselves somewhere in the room.
2. At your signal, the student with the first part of the verse calls out the words several times. The blindfolded volunteer moves toward the student by listening to his or her voice. After finding the first student, the volunteer repeats the process to find the second student.
3. Continue with other volunteers as time permits. Ask: **How can this verse help you live the way God wants you to?**

Option
Print a Bible memory verse on cards, one word per card. Spread out the cards on a table in mixed-up order. Ask a couple blindfolded kids to put the verse cards in order, listening to instructions from other students.

Missing Words

Bible Skill ▸ Bible Verse Memory

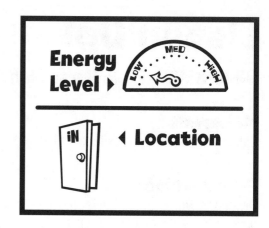

Energy Level ▸

Location ▸

Materials
Bibles, marker, long length of roll paper, index cards, tape

Preparation
Print the words of a Bible memory verse on a large length of roll paper, drawing blank lines for six to eight key words. Print each key word on a separate index card.

Lead the Game
1. Place the index cards and paper you prepared faceup on a table or on the floor. Have kids take turns choosing index cards to place on the blanks on the paper. While taking turns, students can ask classmates if they agree or disagree with the placement of cards. Students may switch or remove cards only if a majority of the class disagrees.
2. After students think they have correctly completed the verse, have students look up the verse in their Bibles. Let them switch cards as needed. Then have kids tape the cards in place. Ask: **How will following the truths of this verse help you love God more?**

Puzzling Words

Bible Skill ▸ Bible Verse Memory

Materials
Bibles, large index cards, red and blue markers, scissors, tape

Preparation
Using a blue marker, write the words of a Bible memory verse on large index cards, two or three words on each card. Using a red marker, print the definitions of several key words in the verse on the backs of the corresponding cards. Cut cards into puzzle pieces and hide the pieces around the room.

Lead the Game
1. Invite students to find the puzzle pieces hidden in the room. Referring to blue letters, students can put the pieces together. Students should then tape the pieces together and put the cards in verse order. As needed, kids can refer to their Bibles.
2. Volunteers can take turns reading the definitions of key words written on the backs of cards. Ask: **What is the most important part of this verse to you?**

Rearranged Verse

Bible Skill ▸ Bible Verse Memory

Energy Level ▸ LOW MED HIGH

◀ Location

Materials
Bibles, paper, marker

Preparation
Print the words of a Bible memory verse on paper, one or two words on each paper.

Lead the Game
1. Divide the class into two groups. One group stands in front of the class, with each student holding one of the verse papers you prepared. Make sure the words are not in order. Tell the other group to find the verse in their Bibles. Kids can take turns giving instructions as to how the students up front should rearrange themselves to be in memory verse order. ("Nathan, take two steps to your right.") If there are more papers than students, let kids arrange just the words of one phrase at a time.
2. Ask all students to read the completed verse aloud together. Then let the other group have a turn up front. When finished, ask: **How can you remember the words of this verse?**

Big Book of Bible Games
for Elementary Kids
© David C Cook. Permission granted to photocopy for ministry purposes only.

Secret Pass

Bible Skill ▶ Bible Verse Memory

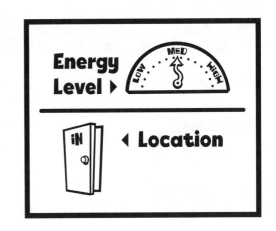

Energy Level ▶

◀ Location

Materials
Bibles, index card, marker, children's music from your collection, music player

Preparation
Print the words of a Bible memory verse on an index card. Think of a question that can be answered by the information given in the verse.

Lead the Game
1. Ask kids to stand in a circle (shoulder-to-shoulder, if possible) to play a game similar to Button, Button, Who's Got the Button? Choose one student to be in the middle. Tell that student to close his or her eyes. Give the verse card to a student in the circle. (Optional: If you have a large group of students, make more than one verse card for students to pass.) Have the student in the middle open his or her eyes.
2. As you play music, students pass the card around the circle behind their backs, trying to keep the student in the middle from seeing who has the card. When you stop the music, the student in the middle tries to identify who has the card by asking a student the question you prepared. If the student does not have the card, he or she answers, "Keep searching." The student in the middle asks another student. If that student does have the card, he or she answers by reading the verse from a Bible. The student with the card goes to the middle. Continue the game as time permits. Ask: **What's the main idea of this verse?**

Sticky Verses

Bible Skill ▶ Bible Verse Memory

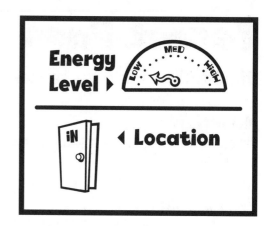

Energy Level ▶

◀ Location

Materials
Bibles, craft sticks, markers

Preparation
Print the words of a Bible memory verse on craft sticks, two or three words on each stick (see sketch). Make one set of sticks for each small group of students. Mix up all the sets together.

Lead the Game
1. Divide the class into small groups. Have each group gather in a circle. Distribute all the prepared craft sticks so each group has an equal amount.
2. Ask students to read the memory verse in their Bibles. Students in each group should arrange their sticks in verse order as much as is possible with the sticks they have Then ask one group to choose a stick to pass to the group on their right (possibly a duplicate). The next group chooses a stick to pass to the group on their right (again, possibly a duplicate). Play continues until a group has the entire verse and puts the sticks in order. Have all students read the memory verse aloud. Ask: **What does this verse mean to you? In what situations would it be good to remember this verse?**

Tape Time

Bible Skill ▸ Bible Verse Memory

Materials
Bibles, masking tape, marker

Preparation
Print the words of a Bible memory verse on masking tape,
with enough space between the words to tear apart the tape.
(If you have a smaller number of students than words in the verse,
print phrases instead of words.) Tear the words apart, and lightly place the separate pieces of tape on the
underside of chairs or tables or on the walls in your room. In the same manner, print a paraphrase of the verse on
masking tape, but do not distribute pieces.

Lead the Game
1. Ask students to find the words you've hidden in the room. After all the words have been found, have kids find
   the memory verse in their Bibles. Then they should put the pieces in order, taping them to the table or floor.
   While students work, put the paraphrase pieces in the room.
2. **Now look for some more words. These words say the memory verse in a slightly different way, which may
   help us understand it better.** When all the pieces have been found, students should work together to put the
   words in order. Ask volunteers to read both the verse and its paraphrase aloud. Ask: **How does the paraphrase
   help you understand the Bible verse better? What is the most important part of this verse to you?**

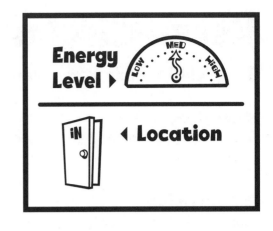

Verse Circles

Bible Skill ▸ Bible Verse Memory

Materials
Bibles, index cards, marker, carpet square (or sheet of construction paper), children's music from your collection, music player

Preparation
Print each word of a Bible memory verse on a separate index card.

Lead the Game
1. Have students form a circle. Place the carpet square or sheet of construction paper between two students so it becomes part of the circle. Mix up the index cards and distribute them.
2. As you play music, kids are to walk around the circle, stepping on the carpet square as they come to it. When you stop the music, the student standing on or near the carpet square should place his or her card on the floor in the middle of the circle. Students holding words before and after the word should put their cards in the correct places.
3. Continue until all cards are in memory verse order. Ask students to read the completed verse together. Ask: **In what situations would it be good to remember this verse? How could you do what this verse says to do?**

Verse Walk

Bible Skill ▸ Bible Verse Memory

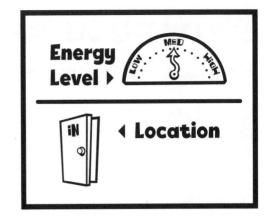

Energy Level ▸

◀ Location

Materials
Bibles, large sheets of paper, marker, self-stick notes, tape, children's music from your collection, music player

Preparation
Print the words of a Bible memory verse on large sheets of paper, two or three words per paper. Place a self-stick note on each paper. Number the phrases in verse order, writing numbers on the self-stick note (see sketch). Tape the papers randomly on the walls.

Lead the Game
1. As you play music, students should walk around the room. When the music stops, each student should place a hand on the nearest paper. More than one student may touch each paper.
2. Students touching the paper with the first phrase should read that phrase aloud. Then the kids touching the second phrase should read that phrase aloud. Continue until the entire verse has been read in the correct order.
3. Repeat the activity. After several rounds, remove the self-stick notes to see if students can remember the order of the words. Ask: **What's the main idea of this verse?**

Writing Relay

Bible Skill ▶ Bible Verse Memory

Energy Level ▶

Location ▶

Materials
Bibles, large sheets of paper, markers, small prizes such as candy or stickers

Preparation
Print the reference for a Bible memory verse at the top of a large sheet of paper—one paper for each group of up to six students. Place papers on one side of the room. Place a marker and a Bible open to the verse next to each paper.

Lead the Game
1. Divide the class into groups of up to six students. Groups should line up opposite of the papers. At your signal, the first student in each line runs to the nearest paper, reads the memory verse from a Bible, and writes the first word of the verse on the paper. That student leaves the Bible open and returns to tag the next person in line. The second student then runs to find and write the second word of the verse. Play continues until one group completes the entire verse.
2. When all the groups have completed the relay, lead kids in reading the verse aloud. Ask: **What do you think this verse means? How could having this verse memorized help you?**

Life Application Games

Faith in God

Faith Encouragers

Bible Focus ▸ 1 Thessalonians 5:11

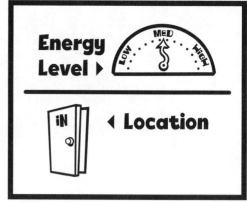

Energy Level ▸

iN ◂ Location

Materials
Bibles, poster board, marker, masking tape, tape measure; for each team of 6 to 7 players: 16 index cards of the same color

Preparation
Print the words of 1 Thessalonians 5:11 on poster board and display. On the floor, use masking tape to mark off a 3' square for each team (see sketch). On one team's index cards, print each word of 1 Thessalonians 5:11, one word or the reference on each card. Use a different color of cards to make an identical set for each team.

Lead the Game
1. **We're going to play a game where we will help each other get an encouraging message.** Draw students' attention to the masking-tape squares on the floor. **These squares are your "homes." To play this game, your team needs to collect all its cards and put the Bible memory verse in order. You can leave your home, but only if you stay connected to someone! Everyone outside the box has to be connected to someone who is inside the box.**
2. Divide the class into teams. Each team stands inside a home. Assign each team one color of index cards. Scatter index cards on the floor at varying distances from the boxes. At your signal, teams should start collecting their index cards by forming an unbroken chain with at least one team member remaining in the home (see sketch). As cards are gathered, they are passed back to the home with team members remaining connected. When all cards have been gathered, the team places the cards on the floor of the home in correct memory verse order. They may refer to the memory verse poster you created or their Bibles. The first team to have the entire verse in order wins. Ask: **In this game, could one person have gathered all the cards alone? Why not?**
3. Ask the winning team to say the verse aloud. Then ask all the kids to say the Bible memory verse together.

Discussion Questions
1. **What does it mean to build up each other?** (to encourage someone, to make someone feel good)
2. **When are times you know a good thing to do, but it's hard to do?**
3. **What are some things you can do to encourage your friends?** (pray for them, offer to help them, help them learn about God and what the Bible says)

Faithful Pitch

Bible Focus ▶ Luke 21:1–4

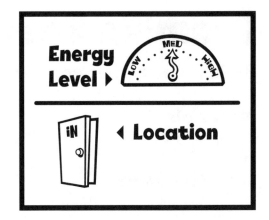

Materials
paper, marker, four metal bowls (or aluminum pie tins), masking tape, coins

Preparation
Print the following words on four sheets of paper, one word per paper: *time*, *money*, *objects*, *obedience*. Arrange bowls and papers as shown (see sketch). Place a masking-tape line about 3' from the bowls.

Lead the Game
1. **The poor widow showed her faith in God by giving Him the last bit of money she had. Let's play a game to show different things we can give to God to show our faith in Him.**
2. Show students the papers you prepared. **These are different kinds of gifts people give. How can we give these gifts to God?** (give time to God by reading the Bible or praying, give money to the church or to people who need it, give objects by sharing what we have with others, give obedience to God by doing what He wants us to do)
3. Give each student several coins. Students should stand behind the masking-tape line and take turns tossing the coins into the bowls. When a coin lands in a bowl, the student tells a way he or she could give to God the kind of gift described on the paper next to the bowl.
4. Play as time permits. Tell students a way you plan to show your faith in God during the week. Invite students to tell ways they will show their faith in God, using the discussion questions as a guide.

Discussion Questions
1. **How can you show your faith in God?** (read about God in His Word, pray to God, thank God for the good things He gives)
2. **When are some times that you've seen other people show their faith in God?** Briefly share an answer before you ask students to respond.
3. **How can you show faith in God when you are with your friends?**

3 feet (9m)

Promise Seekers

Bible Focus ▶ Deuteronomy 7:9

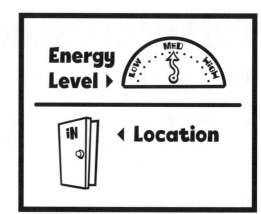

Materials
Bibles, blindfold

Lead the Game
1. Students will play a game similar to Marco Polo. Choose and blindfold a volunteer to be "It." At your signal, students begin walking around the room. "It" calls out "God is faithful to…." The rest of the students respond by saying their names or the names of people they know. "It" follows the voices to try to tag a student.
2. When "It" tags another student, the kid who was tagged answers one of the discussion questions below, says or reads Deuteronomy 7:9 aloud, or describes a situation in which we need to trust in God's faithfulness and His promises. The student who was tagged then becomes "It," and the game continues for as many rounds as time allows.

Option
If you have limited space in which to play the game, have students stand still and whisper names as "It" listens for their voices and tries to tag someone.

Game Tip
Before the game begins, remind students to walk, not run, as they play the game. If you are concerned students will become too active, have everyone except the student who is "It" tiptoe, crawl, or walk in a crouched position.

Discussion Questions
1. **What does Deuteronomy 7:9 tell us about God?** Have a student read the verse aloud.
2. **When might someone your age need to trust in God's faithfulness?** (when feeling afraid, when feeling lonely, when parents fight)
3. **When have you trusted in God's faithfulness? What happened as a result?** You might want to tell your own answer before asking students to respond.

Ship to Shore

Bible Focus ▶ Acts 27

Energy Level ▶

Location

Materials
masking tape, 5 blindfolds, large open playing area

Preparation
Use masking tape to make two lines approximately 10' apart.

Lead the Game
1. **When Paul was traveling to Rome, the ship on which he sailed was destroyed. Paul and his shipmates swam or floated on pieces of the broken ship toward an island. It was a dangerous journey! There were high winds blowing them toward the rocks. They were soaking wet and probably very cold. Let's play a game to see if you can make the dangerous journey from broken ship to sandy shore.**
2. Ask a volunteer to be the "island." The island stands on one side of the playing area. Choose a few students to be "shipmates." The remaining players are "rocks." **What sound should our island make?** Students choose a sound for the island to make, such as slapping thighs to make the sound of waves lapping against shore, or saying "Welcome!" **What sound should the rocks make?** Students choose a sound or words to repeat for waves breaking against the rocks, such as "Crash!" or "Beware of rocks!"
3. Have the rocks spread out around the playing area and sit on the floor, wrapping their arms around their bent knees. Shipmates put on blindfolds at the opposite side of the playing area from the island. At your signal, shipmates attempt to "swim" to the island without running into any rocks. The island makes the island noises to help shipmates find the shore, and the rocks make the rock noises to help the shipmates avoid them. If a shipmate comes in contact with a rock, he or she sits down and becomes a rock. When all shipmates have either become rocks or arrived at the island, choose a new volunteer to be the island. Shipmates and rocks change roles and play is repeated.

Discussion Questions
1. **In the Bible story, when do you think the people on the ship felt afraid?** (when they were blown off course, when the ship started to break up, when the soldiers wanted to kill them, when they were floating in the water)
2. **Why wasn't Paul afraid?** (God promised him that all the people would live. Paul trusted in God's promise.)
3. **How did Paul help his shipmates to keep going, even when it was hard?** (Paul kept reminding them of God's promise to keep them all safe.)

Towel Tug-of-War

Bible Focus ▸ Hebrews 10:23

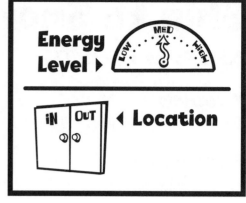

Energy Level ▸

iN OuT ◂ Location

Materials

Bibles, index cards, marker, small paper bag, masking tape, beach towels (or bath towels)

Preparation

Print each Scripture reference on an index card: Deuteronomy 31:6; Isaiah 41:10; Lamentations 3:22–23; Matthew 6:23–31; Romans 8:38–39; 1 Corinthians 10:13; 1 John 1:9. Place the cards in a bag. Place a 1'-strip of masking tape on the floor for every four students.

Lead the Game

1. Stand on one side of the masking-tape line. Invite a student to stand on the other side of the line. Hold onto one end of a towel while the student holds onto the other end. Have a tug-of-war. The first one to pull the other across the tape line reads Hebrews 10:23 from the Bible.

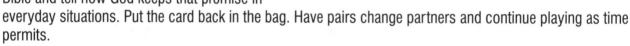

2. Ask students to form pairs. Using a towel, have each pair have a tug-of-war with another pair. The first pair from each group who wins should take a verse card from the bag. Those kids read the verse from the Bible and tell how God keeps that promise in everyday situations. Put the card back in the bag. Have pairs change partners and continue playing as time permits.

Options

1. For a variation, call out a number and have students form two teams of that number.
2. To play outside, use a rope instead of a towel.

Discussion Questions

1. **What does it mean to "hold unswervingly"?** (to hold something without letting go or moving)
2. **What does Hebrews 10:23 tell us to hold onto without giving up?** (our hope in God and His promises)
3. **Why can we do this?** (God is faithful to His promises and always keeps them.)

Life Application Games

Forgiving Others

Forgiveness Balloons

Bible Focus ▸ Genesis 37; 39; 41:41–45

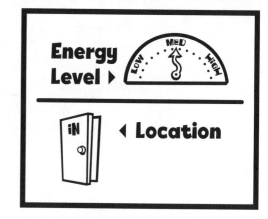

Energy Level ▸

iN ◂ Location

Materials
large balloons (at least 2 per student)

Preparation
none (Optional: inflate and tie balloons before the game)

Lead the Game
1. **We can celebrate the fact that God will always forgive us when we ask Him. His forgiveness helps us want to forgive others. Even when Joseph's brothers treated him very badly, Joseph forgave them. In Bible times, God asked His people to think about their wrong actions during the ten days that are now called the Days of Awe.**
2. Give each kid a balloon to partially inflate and tie. Students should sit close to each other to form circles of no more than six students. Kids are to sit on their inflated balloons. Give each group an additional inflated and tied balloon.
3. Students in each group are to try to tap the balloon to others in their circle ten times. Kids are to tap it in random order, without popping the balloons on which they are sitting. Lead students in counting aloud the number of times the balloon is tapped. If the balloon touches the floor or if a balloon pops, distribute new balloons as needed and let the game begin again. Continue playing as time permits.
4. If you have more than one group, let the groups compete to see which circle can keep the balloon in the air the longest. The winning group earns a letter in the word *forgive*. Continue until one group has earned all the letters or time is up.

Discussion Questions
1. **When has someone forgiven you for doing wrong?**
2. **When might you need to forgive a friend or family member?**
3. **How does remembering God's forgiveness help us forgive others, even when others don't deserve it?**
(We can remember that God forgives us, even when we don't deserve it.)

Forgiveness Find

Bible Focus ▸ Philemon

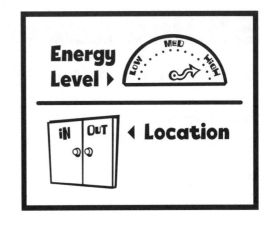

Materials
blindfold

Lead the Game
1. **Because of God's great offer of forgiveness, we can encourage people to forgive each other and make peace. That's why Paul encouraged Philemon to forgive Onesimus. Let's play a game with messages about forgiveness!**
2. Lead students in playing a game like Marco Polo. Blindfold a volunteer to be "It."
3. "It" and the rest of the kids move around the playing area. "It" calls out, "God forgives us." Students respond by saying, "We forgive others." "It" moves toward the students by listening to their voices, continuing to say "God forgives us" to hear students respond.
4. When "It" tags another student, that student becomes "It," and the game begins again.

Options
1. Play the game outdoors, using traffic cones or masking tape to mark the boundaries of the playing area.
2. After several rounds, ask students to think of a new phrase and response about forgiveness. For example, "Forgiveness from God" and "helps us forgive others." Or "We are forgiven" and "so make peace with others."
3. Students stand still while "It" walks around trying to tag them.

Discussion Questions
1. **How do we know God forgives us?** (The Bible tells us God forgives us when we ask for forgiveness. And we know God always keeps His promises.)
2. **Because of God's offer of forgiveness, we should forgive others and encourage people to forgive each other. What are some ways to encourage people to forgive others?** (We can be a good example and forgive others. We can tell others about God's forgiveness.)
3. **How does forgiveness help us make peace?** (When we forgive, we can stop being angry and start doing the right things.)
4. **What might your family be like if no one ever forgave each other? What might your school be like if everyone worked at making peace?**

Sliding Relay

Bible Focus ▸ Genesis 26:1–31; Colossians 3:13

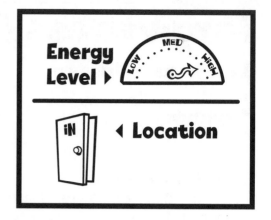

Energy Level ▸

◂ Location

Materials
Bibles, masking tape, large paper plates

Preparation
Use masking tape to make two lines approximately 10' apart.

Lead the Game

1. **Esau's forgiveness of Jacob ended years of angry separation between the two brothers. Let's play a game where we get to think of ways to ask for forgiveness and ways to offer forgiveness to others.**

2. Divide the class into two equal teams. Name the teams "Jacob" and "Esau." Each team should line up behind one of the lines. Give each team two paper plates. At your signal, the first player on each team stands on the paper plates and moves toward the other group's line by sliding his or her feet on the paper plates (see sketch). After reaching the line, the player picks up the paper plates, runs back to his or her team, and hands the paper plates to the next player in line.

3. When both teams have completed the relay, a volunteer from each team stands between the two lines. **Let's pretend one of you lied to the other one. Now you're sorry. Show how you would ask for forgiveness, and how you will offer forgiveness.** Pause as the kids tell what they would do. Ask a volunteer to read Colossians 3:13. Ask: **What does this verse tell us about forgiving others? How do forgiving actions help us make and keep friends?**

4. Continue the relay activity as time permits. Vary the relay by challenging students to move sideways or backwards. Make up other situations in which someone needs to ask for forgiveness and someone needs to offer forgiveness. You can also let kids help make up more situations.

Discussion Questions
1. **Why do you think Esau forgave Jacob?**
2. **What might have happened if Esau had not forgiven Jacob?**
3. **What makes it hard to forgive someone?**

Towel Toss

Bible Focus ▸ The Gospels

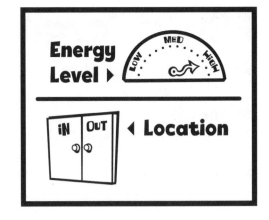

Materials

large towels, balls, whiteboard, dry-erase marker, eraser

Lead the Game

1. **God's great love in sending Jesus to die for our sins is shown to others when we forgive them. Let's play a game to remind us of the importance of forgiveness.**
2. Group students into teams of five. Give each team a towel and a ball.
3. Four students on each team hold the towel at waist height. The other team member stands at a designated spot several feet away and throws the ball so the towel holders can catch it on the towel. If the ball is caught, the thrower runs to the towel and switches places with one of the towel holders. The new thrower takes the ball to the designated area and throws it for the towel holders to catch.
4. Team members continue rotating between throwing and holding. On the board, keep track of the number of times each team catches the ball on the towel. Each time the ball is caught, teams score one letter of the word *forgiveness*. The first team to catch the ball 11 times (completely spelling *forgiveness*) calls "Stop." Students from that team answer one of the discussion questions.

Options

1. If possible, play the game outdoors.
2. Adjust the distance from which students toss the balls according to the students' ages and abilities.
3. For teams with more than five players, students form a line behind the thrower and rotate in.

Discussion Questions

1. **When has someone forgiven you? How did it make you feel?**
2. **Why is it important to forgive other people?** (God wants us to forgive others. It's very important to God we forgive others.)
3. **What might happen when you forgive someone?** (You can be friends again. You can show them God's love.)

Who's Forgiven?

Bible Focus ▶ Matthew 18:21–35

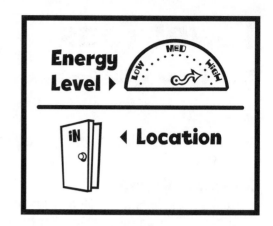

Energy Level ▶

◀ Location

Materials
index cards (1 per student), marker

Preparation
On one index card, print the word *forgiven*. Hide all the cards in the room.

Lead the Game
1. **A long time ago, Jesus told a story about a king and a servant who owed the king lots of money. Let's play a game that reminds us of what the king did.**
2. At your signal, kids should look for the hidden cards. The students with blank cards are debtors (people who owe money) and must do ten jumping jacks or arm circles to pay their debts. The student with the word *forgiven* on his or her card does not have to do jumping jacks or arm circles.
3. Repeat the game as time permits, each time choosing a different way in which debts are to be paid (ten hops across the room, ten toe touches, ten seconds of patting heads and rubbing tummies, and so forth).

Option
If you are unable to hide cards in your room, give each student one of the cards. At your signal, students put their cards facedown and trade with each other. When time is up, students turn their cards over to see who is forgiven and who are debtors.

Discussion Questions
1. **How do you feel when someone says you have done something wrong?**
2. **How do you feel when someone says you are forgiven for what you did?**
3. **Why does God's forgiveness of our sins make us want to forgive others?** (God has been kind to us, so we can be kind to others.)
4. **When might it be hard for you to forgive someone?**
5. **Who helps us forgive others, even when it's hard?**

Life Application Games

Friendship

Balloon Carry

Bible Focus ▸ Ruth

Energy Level ▸ LOW MED HIGH

iN ◂ **Location**

Materials
balloons (1 per pair of students), large bag

Preparation
Inflate and tie the balloons. Place them in a large bag.

Lead the Game
1. **When we make good choices in the things we do and say, we show our faithfulness to God. Sometimes when we make a good choice, it can help our friends and family members. That's what happened when Ruth made a good choice—it helped her mother-in-law, Naomi. Today you and your partner can choose the best way to carry a balloon.**
2. Have students form pairs, and give each pair a balloon. Pairs should stand at one side of the playing area.
3. Tell pairs of students to think about and practice how they can together transport a balloon to the other side of playing area without using their hands to hold the balloon. For example, students could hold the balloon between their shoulders, heads, or hips (see sketch).
4. After students have had time to practice carrying the balloons, ask the pairs to line up on one side of the playing area. Each pair should choose the method of carrying the balloon that they think they can do the best. At your signal, pairs should transport their balloons to the other side of the playing area and back, trying to see who can be the first pair done!

Option
For a greater challenge, increase the number of balloons that the pairs of kids carry.

Discussion Questions
1. **Ruth made the choice to help her mother-in-law, even though it was hard work. How has someone helped you when you had hard work to do?**
2. **Who is someone you can help when they have hard work to do? How?**
3. **What are some ways God helps you when you have hard work to do?** (He gives strength and courage to do it. He listens to and answers prayers.)

Bounce It!

Bible Focus ▸ 1 Timothy 6:18

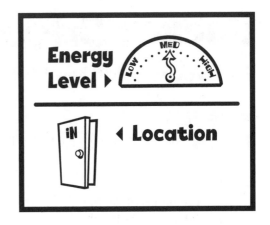

Materials

Bibles, large rubber ball (or tennis ball), children's music from your collection, music player

Lead the Game

1. **Remembering to be kind and generous helps us to make and keep friends. Let's play a game to help us think of some generous and kind actions.**
2. Ask students to stand in a circle and practice bouncing the ball to each other.
3. Have a volunteer read 1 Timothy 6:18 aloud. **What does this verse command us to do?** (do good deeds, be generous, be willing to share) **What are some ways to follow these commands?**
4. When you start the music, students should randomly bounce the ball to each other. When you stop the music, the student with the ball tells a way to obey 1 Timothy 6:18 or says the verse aloud. Continue playing as time allows.

Options

1. Use two balls. Write "2" on one ball and "3" on the other ball. (If needed, numbers could be formed with masking tape.) When you stop the music, students holding the balls should say that number of ways to obey 1 Timothy 6:18.
2. Play a few rounds in which the student holding the ball names a Bible character, a fruit of the Spirit, or a book of the Bible.
3. As students bounce the ball, they should say one word from 1 Timothy 6:18, continuing until the entire verse has been quoted.

Discussion Questions

1. **What are some ways to be generous with others?** (share things with them, give money to help those in need, do service projects in the community)
2. **Why are kind attitudes the best ones for building friendships?**
3. **What actions does the Bible tells us to do?** (love others, honor and obey parents, tell others about God's love)

Bucket Brigade

Bible Focus ▶ Matthew 5:9; Romans 14:19

Energy Level ▶

iN ◀ Location

Materials
Bibles, large disposable cups, 2 tennis balls (or Ping-Pong balls)

Lead the Game
1. **Jesus taught that we are blessed when we make peace. Our friendships are better when we know how to settle arguments and live in peace. Let's play a game to learn an important instruction God gives us about making peace.**
2. Divide the class into two equal teams. Have the teams form parallel lines facing each other.
3. Give each student a cup. Give a tennis ball or ping-pong ball to the student at the end of each line. Those kids should put the balls into their cups.
4. At your signal, the students roll (for mostly younger students) or toss (for mostly older students) the balls to the students across from them. Those students catch the balls in cups and roll or toss the balls to the next students opposite them. Kids continue tossing or rolling the balls in zigzag fashion down the lines (see sketch) and back to the students who began the brigade.

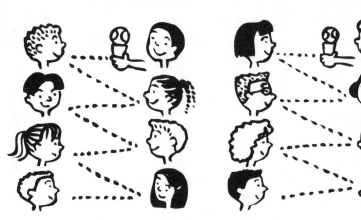

5. Select a volunteer from the team that finished first to answer one of the questions below or repeat Romans 14:19. Keep playing the game as time allows.

Discussion Questions
1. Ask a volunteer to read Romans 14:19 aloud. **What is God's instruction to us in this verse?** ("Make every effort to do what leads to peace.") **What does it mean to "make every effort"?** (to try as hard as you can, to do something to the best of your ability)
2. **What did we make every effort to do in our game?** (catch the ball in our cups, pass the ball to the next player)
3. **How can you make every effort to do what leads to peace at home? At school?** (I could let my brother or sister choose first or borrow something that belongs to me. I could ask God for wisdom about how to treat the person who is bothering me at school. I can be kind to someone who treats me badly.)

Friend Fun

Bible Focus ▸ 1 Samuel 20; Proverbs 17:17

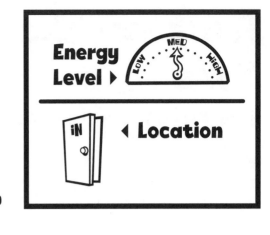

Energy
Level ▸

iN ◂ Location

Materials
Bibles, paper, pencils, timer

Lead the Game
1. **David and Jonathan had a special friendship and showed love to each other. Let's play a fun game to find out some ways we can show love to our friends.**
2. Each student should trace a hand on a sheet of paper.
3. Assign students an action such as "high five," "shake hands" or "pat on the back." Set the timer for 30 seconds. (If you have a larger group, you may want to set the timer for a longer amount of time.)
4. Students are to move around the room and do the assigned action with as many other kids as they can before time is up. When two students have done the action together, they should initial the hands on each other's paper. The goal is to collect as many initials as possible.

5. When time is up, students should count the number of initials on their papers. The kid with the most initials should tell a way to show love to friends. Then let several other volunteers tell ways to show love to friends. Ask for a volunteer to suggest an action for the next round. Students should use the reverse side of the paper (or new sheet of paper if playing more than two rounds) to trace their hands and collect initials for the next round.

Option
Rather than using papers and pencils, students could use washable markers to write initials on each other's hands. When the game is finished, provide moist towelettes for cleaning hands.

Discussion Questions
1. **How do you make friends?** (being friendly to others, listening to others, doing things to help others)
2. Have a volunteer read Proverbs 17:17 aloud. **How has a friend shown love to you?**
3. **What are some other ways that you have shown love to your friends?**

Fruit-of-the-Spirit Toss

Bible Focus ▶ Galatians 5:22–23

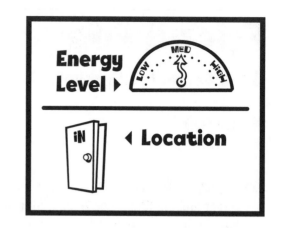

Energy Level ▶

Location ▶ iN

Materials
Bible, balloons (9 per team, plus a few extra), permanent marker, masking tape, bedsheet (1 per team)

Preparation
Inflate the balloons. From Galatians 5:22–23, print one fruit of the Spirit on each balloon. Tape each set of nine balloons to a wall, several feet apart. Spread the bedsheets on the floor across the room, one opposite each group of balloons. In case some balloons pop, have a few more ready to inflate.

Lead the Game
1. **Learning how to live out the qualities of the fruit of the Spirit will help you to be a better friend to others.**
2. Divide the class into teams of up to ten players each. Teams stand in lines, with the first players next to the balloons and the last players near the sheets.
3. At your signal, the first player on each team takes a balloon off the wall, removes the tape, and bats it to the next player in line. While batting the balloons, each student should say the fruit of the Spirit that's written on each balloon. Players should bat the balloons down the line, with the last player batting it onto the sheet. Meanwhile, the first player gets another balloon from the wall and bats it to the next kid in line. The first team to have all its balloons on its sheet wins. If a balloon pops, quickly inflate another balloon, write the fruit of the Spirit on it, and give it to the student who was last holding the popped balloon.

Option
After all the balloons are on the sheets, the kids in each team should pick up their balloons and arrange themselves in verse order.

Discussion Questions
1. **The Bible calls the things written on the balloons the fruit of the Spirit. These are qualities God grows in us as we become more like Jesus. How can these qualities help you be a better friend?**
2. **What are some ways to show these qualities to others?**
3. **What fruit quality do you need most?** You might want to give an example before asking for students' responses.

Partner Relay

Bible Focus ▸ Judges 4:1–16; 5:1–23

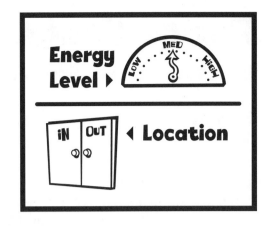

Energy Level ▸

iN OUT ◂ **Location**

Materials
masking tape, newspapers

Preparation
Use masking tape to make a starting line on one side of the playing area.

Lead the Game
1. **Sometimes others need our help to trust God and obey Him. In the Bible we read about how Deborah helped Barak obey God. Let's play a game to practice helping each other.**
2. Divide the class into teams of six to eight players. Have the teams line up behind the masking-tape line. Students on each team should form pairs. Give each pair two sheets of newspaper. (If needed, you can partner with a student and join the fun!)

3. The first student in each line moves across the room and back, stepping only on sheets of newspaper. To do this, the student's partner places newspaper sheets on the floor for his or her partner to walk on. Each pair completes the relay twice, with the other partner moving the newspaper sheets the second time.
4. Keep playing the game as time permits, forming new teams and new pairs.

Options
1. Instead of newspapers, you could use large lengths of roll paper.
2. You could play this game outdoors. Use yarn or string to mark the starting line.

Discussion Questions
1. **How can you help a friend who has something hard to do?** (pray for my friend, offer to help my friend)
2. **When has someone helped or encouraged you to obey God? How?**

Peace Practice

Bible Focus ▶ Colossians 3:15

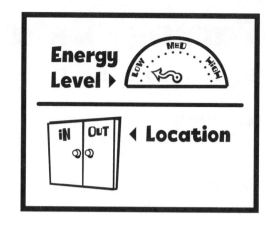

Energy Level ▶

iN OuT ◀ Location

Materials
Bibles

Lead the Game
1. **Being able to make peace with your friends is something that will help you to be a better friend. Let's play a game to work together and spell the word** *peace.*
2. Divide the class into two teams.
3. Tell students on each team to work together to figure out how to spell *peace* by using their bodies. Depending on the number of kids on each team, each student could form a letter or work with a partner or two to form a letter. Make sure that all the kids find a way to participate.
4. When the teams are ready, ask one of the teams to go first and show how they spell the word *peace.* Tell them to freeze and hold that position. Then ask the team to answer two of the discussion questions. Then that team can unfreeze.
5. Have the other team do the same. After they've spelled "peace" with their bodies, tell them to freeze and hold that position. Then ask the team to answer two of the discussion questions.

Options
1. Mix up the teams and tell them to try new ways of using their bodies to spell *peace.*
2. Give each team a long length of roll paper. Tell them to creatively write *peace* on their papers.

Discussion Questions
1. **What does Colossians 3:15 say should rule in the hearts of those who are Christians?** ("the peace of Christ")
2. **When are some times kids your age have to work to make peace at school? At home?** (when friends are arguing, when brothers or sisters are angry)
3. **Why might you gain friends when you work to make peace?** (Most people like to be around those who are friendly and easy to get along with.)

Big Book of Bible Games for Elementary Kids

Quick-Slow Switch

Bible Focus ▸ James 1:19; 3:3–12

Energy Level ▸

iN | OuT ◀ Location

Materials
Bibles, masking tape

Preparation
On the floor, use masking tape to form three large squares.

Lead the Game
1. **Being careful about what we say shows self-control and helps us to be better friends to others. James 1:19 tells us to be "quick to listen, slow to speak and slow to become angry." Let's practice being quick and slow in our game today.**
2. Ask a volunteer to be "It." Form three groups from the remaining students. Each group needs to stand in one of the squares.
3. Call out either "quick" or "slow" and a description, such as "kids wearing green" or "kids with brown hair." Students who fit that description should move to a new square at the speed you called out. "It" also moves at the same speed, trying to tag students before they reach a new square. The first student who is tagged outside a square becomes "It."
4. Continue playing the game, periodically calling out "quick switch" or "slow switch." When kids hear either of these instructions, all students must move at the designated speed to a new square. When only a few students have not been tagged, begin another round of the game with a new "It."

Options
1. Each time you call out a new description, play fast or slow music to indicate the speed at which students should move.
2. To challenge older students, review James 1:19 and then say "listen" to indicate quick movement and "speak" to indicate slow movement during the game.

Discussion Questions
1. **When might it be hard to show self-control when you talk to others?** (when I'm angry, when I feel like saying something unkind, when I don't like what someone is saying)
2. **What can you do when you need help showing self-control in your speech?** (I can remember what James 1:19 says about being quick to listen and slow to speak. I can pray and ask God for His help. I can count to ten before I speak and think about what I will say. I could walk away before I say something I shouldn't.)
3. **How would your school be a better place if everyone did what James 1:19 said to do?**

Teamwork

Bible Focus ▶ Nehemiah 1–4, 8–9

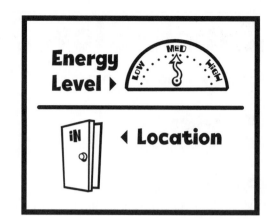

Materials
1 chair for each student, plus an extra chair; 2 sealed bags of individually wrapped candy

Preparation
Arrange chairs so the teams face each other with at least 12' between the teams. Place a chair in the middle (see sketch).

Lead the Game
1. **Working together to do a job usually makes the job easier and it's more fun. Let's play a fun game in which we need to work together so we can each have a piece of candy.**
2. Group students into two equal teams, and ask the teams to sit together in the chairs you've set up. Give the sealed bag of candy to the first student at the left end of each team. At your signal, the first student from each team should run around the center chair to the end of his or her team's chairs. While the student is running, the other students move up one seat to fill the runner's chair, leaving the chair at the right

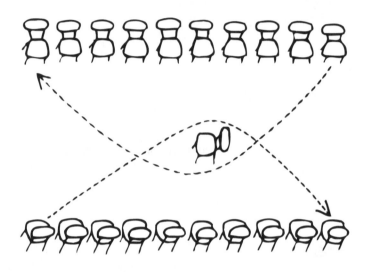

end empty for the runner. The runner sits in the empty chair and passes the bag of candy up the line toward the first chair. When the student sitting in the first chair receives the candy bag, he or she gets up, runs around the center chair, and goes back to the end of the line where the chair is again vacant because the students have moved up one chair. The runner passes the bag of candy up the line again. The team whose players are sitting in their original chairs first is the winner. Then let kids enjoy some candy.

Discussion Questions
1. **In the Bible, we read about a time when Nehemiah helped God's people rebuild the walls around Jerusalem. What made it a hard and difficult job?** (the walls had been broken down for a long time, there were people who made fun of Nehemiah and the others as they worked)
2. **When are some times that you've had a hard job to do? What could have made it easier?**
3. **When you work with others, how can you show good teamwork?** (by being patient and kind, by doing the best that I can)

Life Application Games

God's Forgiveness

Favorite Things

Bible Focus ▸ Luke 15:1–2,11–32

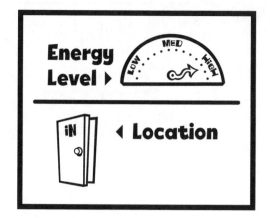

Energy Level ▸

◂ Location

Materials
Bibles

Lead the Game
1. **The Bible teaches us that God is eager to forgive us. Let's play a game to show some things we are eager or excited about.**
2. Ask kids to stand in the middle of the room. As you ask the questions listed here, point to the opposite walls of the room as you say each answer. Each student walks quickly and touches the wall that indicates his or her answer. Questions: **What's your favorite food to eat—ice cream or cookies? What's your favorite game to play— baseball or soccer? What's your favorite thing to do—play video games or play with a friend? What's your favorite thing to ride— a bike or a skateboard? What's your favorite thing to do with your family—go to a park or go out to eat? What's your favorite pet—a cat or a dog?** Ask additional questions, playing as many rounds as time allows. (Note: Students with an answer other than the two given can raise their hands. You can call on a few kids to say how they would answer the question.)

Options
1. Let an older student ask the questions or suggest additional questions.
2. Alternate the way in which students move during this game. Instead of walking quickly to a wall, kids could hop, skip, walk backwards, tiptoe, and so forth.

Discussion Questions
1. **What does it mean to be eager?** (to be so excited about something you want to do it right away, to look forward to something)
2. **Jesus told a story in the Bible about a father who was eager to forgive his son.** You may want students to read Luke 15:11–24. **What is God eager to do for us?** (God is eager to love us. God is eager to forgive us when we do wrong things.)
3. **How does it make you feel to know that God is eager to love you and forgive you? Since God forgives us, how should we treat others?**

Forgiveness Frenzy

Bible Focus ▸ Luke 19:1–10

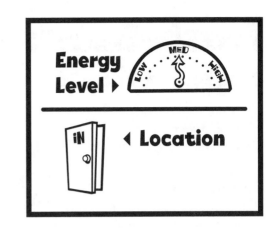

Materials
Bibles, markers, index cards, children's music from your collection, music player

Preparation
Print each letter in the word *forgive* on its own index card. Make at least one set of cards for every three to six students. Mix up all the cards, and place them facedown in a large circle on the floor.

Lead the Game
1. **Let's play a game to celebrate the fact that God's forgiveness is offered to everyone!**
2. Form teams of three to six students. Assign a name or number to each team. Members of all teams should stand in mixed-up order around the circle of cards.
3. As you play music, students are to walk around the circle. Stop the music after ten seconds or so. When the music stops, each student should pick up the card closest to him or her and then get together with all his or her team members. The team members are to compare the cards they are holding, keeping the cards with letters needed to spell *forgive*. They should place duplicate cards facedown, back in the circle. Add blank cards to the circle as needed so that there is always a card for each student.
4. When one or more teams have collected a complete set of cards that spells *forgive*, ask one or more of the discussion questions below. As time allows, keep playing the game.

Options
1. If you have fewer than six students in your class, students can form pairs or play individually.
2. For older students, add a few cards with letters not used in the word *forgive*.

Discussion Questions
1. **What are some things people might think they have to do in order to be forgiven of their sins?** (go to church, read the Bible) **Those are all good things to do, but who does Acts 10:43 say will have their sins forgiven?** (those who believe in Jesus)
2. **What does it mean to believe in Jesus?** (to believe that Jesus is God's Son and that He died to take the punishment for our sins)
3. **How can we know that our sins are forgiven?** (God always keeps His promises; see 1 John 1:9.)

Fresh-Start Tag

Bible Focus ▸ 1 John 1:9

Energy
Level ▸

iN OuT ◂ Location

Materials
Bibles, masking tape (or chalk), party horn

Preparation
Make two masking-tape lines about 30' apart. Make each line at least 10' long. Use chalk if you are playing on asphalt.

Lead the Game
1. **When God forgives the wrong things we have done, we can make a new start. We're going to play a game in which we can practice making new starts!**
2. Choose one volunteer to be "It." "It" stands between the two lines. All other students stand behind one line.
3. **In the Old Testament, when God wanted to get the Israelites' attention, the priests blew the shofar, a ram's horn, like a trumpet. In our game today, the horn is your signal to run back and forth between the two masking-tape lines without getting tagged.** Blow the horn. Students are to run to the opposite line, trying not to be tagged by "It." Students who are tagged stay in the middle and help "It" tag other students. Students who have not been tagged continue running back and forth between the two masking-tape lines. When most students have been tagged (or after several minutes of play), blow the horn again and say, "Forgiven!" All the students who were tagged get to make a new start and be runners again. Choose a new volunteer to be "It." Repeat the game as time allows.

Options
1. If space is limited, students could jump or hop between the two lines.
2. If possible, play the game outdoors.

Discussion Questions
1. **What happened when I said the word *forgiven*?** (The game started over. Everyone got a new chance to be a runner.) **How is that like what happens when God forgives us?**
2. **When are some other times we get to make a new start?** (begin a new school year, begin reading a new book, begin playing a higher level on a video game)
3. Have a volunteer read 1 John 1:9. **How do we confess our sins to God?** (We talk to God about the wrong things we've done and ask Him to forgive us.)

God's Amazing Plan

Bible Focus ▸ 1 Corinthians 2:9

Energy Level ▸

Location ▸

Materials
Bibles, masking tape, blindfold

Preparation
Use masking tape to divide the playing area into four sections (see sketch).

Lead the Game
1. **The Bible tells us in 1 Corinthians 2:9 that no eye has seen or ear has heard "the things God has prepared for those who love Him." Let's play a game and talk about the good things God wants to give us!**
2. Choose one volunteer to be blindfolded and one volunteer to be "It." The blindfolded volunteer stands in the middle of the playing area.
3. At your signal, "It" and the remaining students move randomly (but quietly) around the playing area. The blindfolded volunteer counts to 20 and then says, "Stop!" All students freeze where they are, and the volunteer points toward one of the playing-area sections. If "It" is in that section, "It" reads 1 Corinthians 2:9 aloud or answers one of the discussion questions. If "It" is not in that section, all students in that section move to the side of the playing area. Keep playing until the blindfolded volunteer points to the section where "It" is standing. As time allows, play again with new volunteers.

Option
If you have a large number of students, choose more than one "It" for each round of the game.

Discussion Questions
1. **What are some good things God gives His followers?** (forgiveness of sins, courage to do right, the promise to always be with us)
2. **What are some good things God promises to help you do?** (treat others fairly, be patient and kind to others, love others)
3. **When are some times that it's hard to live as God wants us to? What can you do then?** (I can pray and ask for God's help. I can read the Bible for encouragement.)

Jonah's Journey

Bible Focus ▶ Jonah; 1 Timothy 2:3–4

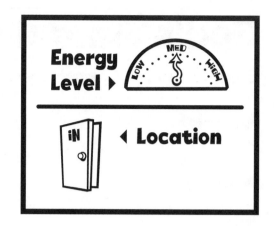

Energy Level ▶

◀ **Location**

Materials
Bibles, markers, length of roll paper, masking tape, index cards, blindfold

Preparation
Draw outlines of a whale (or big fish) and the city of Nineveh on roll paper (see sketch). Then tape the paper to a wall.

Lead the Game
1. **In the Old Testament, Jonah went on an unusual journey. As a result, people learned about God's forgiveness.** Invite volunteer(s) to tell the story of Jonah's journey to Nineveh.
2. **Let's play a game to remind us of Jonah's journey.** On an index card, each student is to draw a stick figure to represent Jonah, then attach a masking-tape loop to the back of the card.

3. Have kids line up approximately 5' from the paper you've prepared. Blindfold the first volunteer, and spin him or her three times. The student should walk to the roll paper and attach his or her card to the paper. Continue until all kids have had a turn. Ask the student who placed his or her card closest to Nineveh to answer one of the discussion questions below or to say or read 1 Timothy 2:3–4.

Option
If you have more than six to eight students, make additional papers. Students can play the game in small groups.

Discussion Questions
1. **How can we stop doing wrong things?** (We can tell God we're sorry, and ask Him to help us do what's right. We can read and study the Bible more to know what God wants us to do.)
2. **How do we know our sins are forgiven?** (The Bible tells us if we ask God for forgiveness for the wrong things we have done, we will be forgiven.)
3. **What are some ways we can learn the right things God wants us to do?** (We can study God's Word. We can attend church services. We can listen to and follow the instructions of people who love God.)

Shoe Search

Bible Focus ▶ Luke 15:1–10

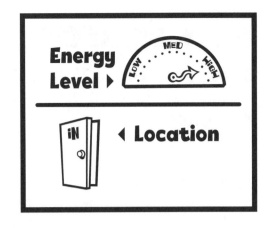

Materials
Bibles

Lead the Game
1. **When we find something we've been looking for, it makes us happy. In Luke 15, Jesus told two stories about people who searched for missing items.** (Optional: Read Luke 15:1–10 aloud.) **When the people found the missing items, they were happy! Let's search for something in our game today.**
2. Have kids form two teams. Students on each team are to take off their shoes and place them in a team pile on one side of the playing area. Students should line up in single-file lines on the other side of playing area, across from their team's shoe pile. Mix up the shoes in each pile.
3. At your signal, the first student in line on each team is to skip to the shoe pile, find one of his or her shoes, put it on, and skip back to his or her team. The next student in line repeats the action. Students continue taking turns until everyone on the teams have collected and put on both shoes.

Option
You could use this game to review Habakkuk 3:18. Stand by one pile of shoes and have a helper stand by the other pile. When a student comes to the shoe pile, begin reading the verse. Stop at any point. The student is to finish the verse, then take a shoe from the pile and return to the team.

Discussion Questions
1. **What are some ways people hear about God's gift of salvation and the joy it brings?** (Friends or family members tell them. They go to church services. They read the Bible.)
2. **When we hear about God and accept His gift of salvation, we experience joy. Why?** (We know our sins are forgiven by God. We know that we will have eternal life in heaven with God.)
3. **The Bible tells us God rejoices when we become a part of His family. Why?** (He loves us and wants us to be part of His family. He created us and wants to spend eternity with us.)

Son Search

Bible Focus ▶ Luke 15:11–24

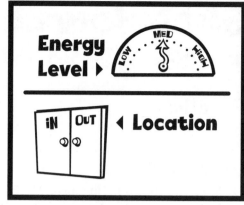

Energy Level ▶

Location ▶

Materials
blindfold

Lead the Game
1. **When we're sorry for the wrong things we've done, God is always ready to forgive us. To help us learn about God's love and forgiveness, Jesus told a story in Luke 15:11–24 about a loving and forgiving father. Let's play a game to remember that story and think about God's great love and forgiveness!**
2. **In the story Jesus told, a son left home and spent all his money on parties. He was so poor that he got a job taking care of pigs. The son finally decided to go home and ask his father to forgive him for his wrong actions. His father was glad to welcome him home!** (Optional: Invite volunteers to tell what they remember about the story.)
3. Lead students in playing a game like Marco Polo. Blindfold a volunteer; that student is the father. Choose another volunteer to be the son. The rest of the students are the pigs.
4. The father begins calling out, "Welcome home, Son." The son responds by saying, "I'm sorry, Father" while walking slowly around the playing area. While moving around the playing area, the rest of the students oink and snort like pigs. The father moves toward the son by listening for his or her response while continuing to say, "Welcome home, Son." When the father tags the son or after several minutes, choose two new volunteers to be the father and son. Continue the game as time allows.

Options
1. Be sure to clear the playing area of tables and chairs. If you play the game outdoors, use yarn to indicate boundaries.
2. If playing the game with younger students, the kids representing the son and the pigs could stand still while the father tries to find the son.

Discussion Questions
1. **When does God forgive us?** (God forgives us when we are sorry for our sins and ask Him to forgive us.)
2. **When is a good time to ask God to forgive us?** (whenever we realize we have sinned, whenever we're sorry for the wrong things we've done and want to start doing right things)
3. **What are some ways to celebrate and thank God for the forgiveness He offers?** (thank Him when we pray, forgive others, tell others about God's forgiveness)

Big Book of Bible Games
for Elementary Kids
© David C Cook. Permission granted to photocopy for ministry purposes only.

Life Application Games

God's Help

Alphabetical Help

Bible Focus ▸ Philippians 4:19

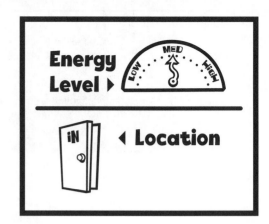

Energy Level ▸ LOW MED HIGH

iN ◂ Location

Materials
Bibles, masking tape, large sheets of paper, markers

Preparation
Use masking tape to make a starting line on one side of the room. Print the alphabet down one side of the paper, making one paper for each group of up to eight students. Place the alphabet papers and markers on the opposite side of the room.

Lead the Game
1. Divide the class into teams of up to eight students each. Teams are to line up behind the starting line. Each team sends one person at a time to its large sheet of paper. Kids are to write a name of something God made next to the letter of the alphabet with which the name begins. Call time after several minutes.
2. The team with the most words on its alphabet paper chooses one thing on their paper. Ask that team the discussion questions below. Then do the same with the other teams. Ask students to find Philippians 4:19 in their Bibles, and have a volunteer read the verse aloud. **How does this verse say God takes care of us?** (He meets all our needs.)

Option
You can play the game again, but use different categories of items God uses to meet our needs (food, things to drink, plants, animals, friends and family members, and so forth).

Game Tips
When putting students in groups, make sure that there is at least one good reader and/or writer in each group. And don't worry about words being spelled correctly. The most important part of this game is seeing how God helps us and meets our needs.

Discussion Questions
1. **Why do you think God made this thing?**
2. **How does this thing help us?**
3. **What are other ways God helps us?** (God helps us when we're afraid or lonely. God helps us when we face bullies. God helps us to forgive others.)

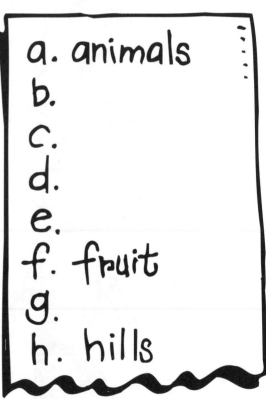

a. animals
b.
c.
d.
e.
f. fruit
g.
h. hills

Balance Relay

Bible Focus ▶ Psalm 55:16–17

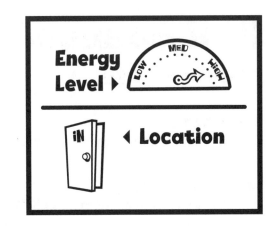

Energy Level ▶

◀ **Location**

Materials

Bibles, paper cups and plates, marker

Preparation

Divide Psalm 55:16–17 into six sections. Print each section and the reference on a cup or plate, alternating cups and plates (sketch a). Make one set for each group of no more than six students.

Lead the Game

1. Divide the class into teams of no more than six students each. Each team should line up, half on one side of the room and half on the other side of the room (sketch b). Set out plates and cups as shown.
2. At your signal, the first player on each team finds the plate with the first phrase from Psalm 55:16–17. That player carries the plate to other side of the room and gives the plate to the first player in that line. This player finds the cup with the second phrase from the verse, places it on the plate, and carries the cup and plate across the room, giving them to the next player in line. Play continues until all the cups and plates are stacked together in the proper order. If plates and cups fall, students should restack them and continue carrying them to the other side of the room.
3. The first team to finish reads Psalm 55:16–17 aloud together, then answers a discussion question.

Options

1. Teams could sit together at tables and compete to see which team is the first to stack cups and plates in verse order.
2. If the game seems too easy, add the rule that only one hand can be used to carry the cups and the plates.

Discussion Questions

1. **When does Psalm 55:16–17 say God will hear us?** Have students read these verses in their Bibles.
2. **When are some times kids your age might ask God for help?** (when studying for a test, when afraid of something, when feeling sad)
3. **How could talking to God about our problems help?** (It can remind us that God knows what is best for us. It shows that we are putting our trust in God. It can help us think differently about our problems.)

Ball Bounce

Bible Focus ▶ Ruth

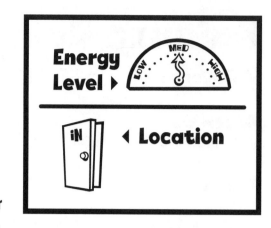

Energy Level ▶

◀ Location

Materials
container (wastebasket, large bowl, cardboard box), ball

Lead the Game
1. **In the Bible we read the story of Ruth. Ruth helped and cared for someone in her family. God gives us people who care for us too. Let's play a game to think of some of those people!**
2. Students line up approximately 3' from the container.
3. Students take turns bouncing a ball at least once while attempting to get the ball into the container. When the ball goes into the container, the student tells the name of someone who cares for him or her. If the ball does not go into the container after three tries, the next student takes a turn. Continue play as time allows.

Options
1. Consider the age and ability of your students and adjust the distance students stand from the container.
2. If you have more than six students in your group, provide additional balls and containers in order to limit the time kids spend waiting in line.

Discussion Questions
1. **How does (your mother) care for you? How does (your teacher) care for you?** Repeat with other people named by students.
2. **How do you care for others?**

Balloon Bat

Bible Focus ▶ Mark 4:35–41

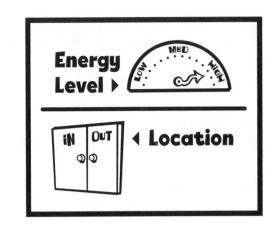

Energy Level ▶

Location ◀

Materials
masking tape, ruler, inflated and tied balloon, chair (or cone)

Preparation
Tear off 3" strips of tape (two per student). Place a chair or cone, representing the goal, at one end of the playing area.

Lead the Game
1. **In Mark 4, we read about a time when Jesus' disciples were in a difficult situation. They were in danger of drowning in a storm. What did the disciples discover?** (They found out they could count on Jesus to help them.) **No matter how bad things seem or how stuck we feel in certain situations, we can depend on God because He's in control and promises to help us. Let's play a game in which we're stuck in one place but we can still help each other!**
2. Students should stand evenly scattered in the playing area. Each student tapes a masking-tape X where he or she is standing.
3. Bat the balloon into the playing area at the opposite end from the goal. Students should begin batting the balloon toward the goal, keeping one foot on their Xs at all times. Each student must touch the balloon at least once, and if the balloon touches the floor, the game restarts. After the balloon goes past the goal, begin a new round by batting the balloon into the playing area again.

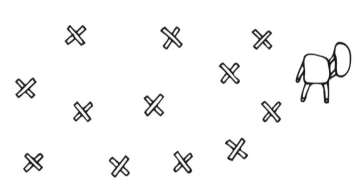

Options
1. Adjust the size of the playing area according to the number of students, making sure that students stand at least an arm's distance away from each other. If playing in a small area, students could keep both feet on their Xs at all times.
2. This game could be played outside on a paved area. Students use chalk to draw Xs.

Discussion Questions
1. **Even when we are worried about something or feel stuck in certain situations, we can believe God is able to help us. What can you do to depend on God's help during hard times?** (pray and ask for His help, believe God will help, ask other people who love God for their help)
2. **Why can we depend on God to help us?** (He made us and cares about us. He promises to helps us and God always keeps His promises.)
3. **How has God helped you or your family in the past? How do you need God's help today?**

Balloon Fears

Bible Focus ▸ Exodus 13:17—15:21

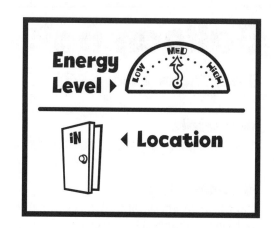

Energy Level ▸

◂ Location

Materials
Bibles, masking tape, balloons, 2 pushpins

Preparation
Mark two masking-tape squares on the floor, approximately 8' to 10' apart. Each square should be large enough for a student to stand in.

Lead the Game
1. **God freed the Israelites from Egyptian slavery. But as the Israelites came to the Red Sea, the Egyptian army raced toward them. The people were probably afraid. But God parted the sea and all the Israelites crossed over safely. Let's play a game in which we talk about being afraid.**
2. Divide the class into two teams. Each team chooses a captain who stands in one of the squares. Give each captain a pushpin. Team members should kneel on the floor in the playing area between the two captains, positioning themselves evenly throughout the playing area and facing toward the middle of the playing area. No one other than the captain may enter a captain's square.
3. Blow up and tie a balloon. Tap the balloon above the heads of the teams. Team members, while remaining on their knees, try to tap the balloon toward their own captain so he or she can catch and pop the balloon with a pushpin. (If you need students to be a little calmer while playing this game, add the rule that they must not only stay on their knees, but also must keep one hand on the floor at all times.) When the balloon is popped, a volunteer from the team who popped the balloon answers one of the discussion questions.
4. Continue the game as time permits with new balloons and different captains for each round of play. When time is up, lead students in a brief time of prayer, inviting volunteers to thank God for His love and help.

Discussion Questions
1. **How might the words of Exodus 15:11 help someone who is afraid?** Have a volunteer read the verse aloud.
2. **When might the kids you know feel worried or afraid?**
3. **How can God help you with your fears?** (I can remember how great and powerful God is and trust that He will help me. I can talk to God about my fears. God might help me through a friend or family member.)

Battle of Jericho

Bible Focus ▸ Joshua 1, 3, 6

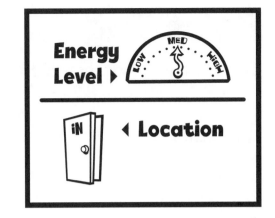

Energy Level ▸ LOW MED HIGH

iN ◂ **Location**

Materials
children's music from your collection; music player; 1 chair for each student, minus one; wooden (or cardboard) blocks

Preparation
Place chairs in a circle, facing out. Several feet away from the chairs, stack blocks to make a wall.

Lead the Game
1. **No matter how hard things are, God is always there to help us. When the Israelites faced Jericho, they needed God's help. Let's play a game to act out what happened in this Bible story.**
2. Have kids walk around the chairs as you play music.
3. When you stop the music, each student tries to sit in a chair. The student without a chair removes one of the blocks from the wall. Continue playing until the wall has been dismantled. Talk about how the walls of Jericho didn't come down one block at a time but that God caused the walls to collapse all at once. As time permits, play additional rounds of the game.

Option
If blocks are not available, draw a block wall on the board. Students can erase blocks as the game is played.

Discussion Questions
1. **When are some times you've needed God's help?**
2. **Why might someone forget to depend on God?**
3. **God provides people to help us. If you needed help, what could someone do or say to help you in different situations?**

Boat Tag

Bible Focus ▸ Matthew 8:23–27; Mark 4:35–41; Luke 8:22–25; John 14:27

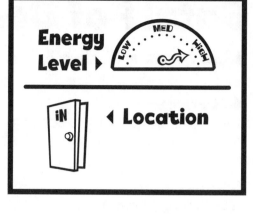

Materials
masking tape

Preparation

On the floor, use masking tape to form at least two shapes representing boats large enough to fit the number of students in your class. (For example, if you have 20 students, make four boats large enough for five students to stand in each shape.) Space shapes 5' apart.

Lead the Game

1. **Because God's power is greater than anything, He can help us when we're afraid. Jesus' disciples learned about His power when they were in boats during a big storm, and Jesus made the storm stop. Let's play a game that reminds us of Jesus' power.**
2. Ask a volunteer to be "It." Form at least two groups from the remaining students. Each group should stand in a separate boat marked on the floor.
3. One at a time, call out a description such as "kids wearing red" or "kids in second grade." Students who fit a description run to a new boat while "It" tries to tag them before they are inside their new boats. Any student who is tagged also becomes "It." Continue playing, periodically calling out, "Boats are sinking," at which all students must run to new boats. When only a few students have not been tagged, begin a new round of the game with a new "It."

Options

1. If you have a large group, choose more than one student to be "It."
2. If indoor space is limited, play this game outside on a paved area. Draw the boats with chalk.

Discussion Questions

1. **What are some powerful things kids your age might be afraid of?** (storms, earthquakes, tornadoes)
2. **Why can God help us when we're afraid of these things?** (God created everything, and He is more powerful than anything He created. God loves us and wants to help us.)
3. **How does God help us when we are afraid?** (He answers our prayers. He gives us adults to help us feel safe. He helps us remember His power. He gives us courage and peace.)

Care-Full Question

Bible Focus ▶ Mark 5:21–43; Luke 8:40–56

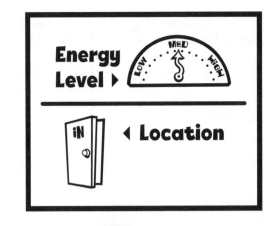

Energy Level ▶ LOW MED HIGH

IN ◀ Location

Materials
large piece of paper, marker, masking tape, blindfold

Lead the Game

1. **In the Bible we read a story about a time when Jesus cared for a sick woman and a young girl who had died. God knows us and helps us with our needs too. One way God helps us is by providing people who care for us. Let's play a game to name some of the people who help take care of us.**

2. Have kids name specific people who care for them. List students' responses on the paper. Display the paper for kids to refer to during the game.

3. Ask students to stand in a circle. Choose a volunteer to stand in the middle of the circle, and blindfold the volunteer. Tell students standing in the circle to begin walking clockwise. When the blindfolded volunteer stomps his or her feet twice, students stop moving. The volunteer is to point in any direction and say, "Good morning, Mr. Brown. Who cares for you?" (Note: The volunteer can substitute any last name for "Brown.")

4. The student to whom the volunteer pointed should respond by saying, "(My parents) care for me." Remind kids that, as needed, they can refer to the list made earlier. If the volunteer in the middle can identify the speaker, they change places. If not, play another round. If the volunteer does not identify the speaker after two rounds, allow another student to have a turn in the middle.

Option
Before the game, review students' names by grouping students in pairs and asking each student to introduce his or her partner to the whole group. Or play the game in groups of no more than eight so students will be able to easily remember each others' names.

Discussion Questions
1. **How have some of the people we talked about in the game cared for you?**
2. **As you grow older, how do you think parents and teachers will continue to care for you?** (They will help me learn to do new things like driving a car. They will help me choose which college to attend.)
3. **What can you do this week to thank someone who cares for you?**

Colorful Costumes

Bible Focus ▶ Genesis 37, 39–45

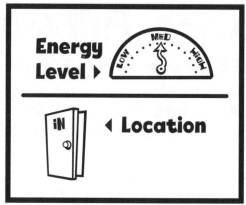

Energy Level ▶

◀ Location

Materials
rolls of tape, colored newspaper comics, colored construction paper, colored tissue paper

Lead the Game
1. **Receiving a coat of many colors was the beginning of a long adventure for Joseph. There were times when Joseph had to go through hard times in that adventure, but God was always with him. We're going to have an adventure making our own colorful coats!**
2. Divide the class into groups of no more than four students each. Give each group a roll of tape and some comics, construction paper, and tissue paper.
3. Each group is to choose one student to dress in a paper coat they will make. Kids can make the coats by taping the different kinds of paper together. Each coat must have a front, a back, and two sleeves.

Options
1. If you have older students, they could compete to see which group can make the best paper coat in five minutes.
2. Invite students wearing coats to participate in a fashion show. Group members can describe the coats as students model them.

Discussion Questions
1. **No matter what happened to him, Joseph knew and always remembered God was with him. When are some times kids your age need to remember God is with them?**
2. **When has God helped you or your family in the past?**
3. **When do you need to remember God's love and help?**

Big Book of Bible Games for Elementary Kids

© David C Cook. Permission granted to photocopy for ministry purposes only.

Frisbee Bowling

Bible Focus ▸ Exodus 16:1—17:7

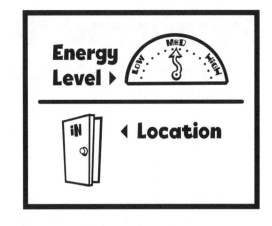

Energy Level ▸ LOW MED HIGH

iN ◂ Location

Materials
paper cups, markers, Frisbee

Lead the Game
1. **As God's people moved through the desert, He provided a bread-like food called manna to fall from the sky. The people always had enough to eat. God continues to give us what we need. Let's play a game to remember the good things God provides for us.**
2. **What are some needs people have?** (air, food, water, place to live, family, friends, clothes) Print each category on a separate paper cup. On one side of the room, set up cups like bowling pins (see sketch).
3. Ask kids to stand in a line at least 6' from the cups. Students are to take turns rolling the Frisbee on its edge toward the cups. When a student knocks over a cup, that student is to name one specific thing that God has given him or her from the category written on that cup. (Example: family—mom, grandpa, sister) The student should then place the cup back in the correct position. Keep playing as time allows.

Options
1. Instead of paper cups, collect empty soda cans or plastic liter bottles. Print categories on separate index cards and tape cards to the cans or bottles.
2. Make one set of cups for every six to eight students. Set up bowling areas for each group of students.
3. Adjust the distance from which students roll the Frisbee according to the age of the kids. Older students could stand farther back than younger students.
4. If kids are knocking down all or most of the cups with one roll of the Frisbee, spread the cups farther apart.

Discussion Questions
1. **What are some times in the Bible when God gave people what they needed?** (When the Israelites were in the desert, God gave manna and water to them. When Pharaoh was chasing the Israelites, God parted the Red Sea for them. God gave instructions to Noah to build an ark so he and his family would be safe during the flood.)
2. **With the things God has given us, how can He use us to help provide for other people's needs?** (We can share what we have with others. We can help serve food to people at a homeless shelter. We can give our offerings at church, so the church can use the money to help people with their needs.)

Numbered Needs

Bible Focus ▸ Mark 2:1–12; Luke 5:17–26; Philippians 4:19

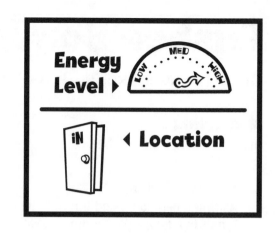

Energy Level ▸

◂ **Location**

Materials
Bibles, sock (or eraser), whiteboard, dry-erase marker

Lead the Game

1. **Jesus healed a man who couldn't walk when the man's friends brought him to Jesus. No matter what we need, we can depend on God to help and care for us. Let's play a game in which we race to get something we need!**

2. Play a game like Steal the Bacon. Divide the class into two equal teams. Each team stands in a straight line facing the other team, leaving about 10' between the teams. One team numbers off from one end of the line, while the other team numbers off from the opposite end (see sketch).

3. Hold up the sock or eraser. **We're going to pretend this is something we need. What is something we need that this (sock) could represent?** (water, food, air, warm clothes, shelter) Choose one of those things for the (sock) to represent. Place the (sock) in the center of the playing area, reminding students what it represents.

4. Call a number. Kids on both teams with that number run to grab the item in the center. The student who gets the item first runs back to his or her team. The student who does not get the item tells a new need that the item could represent for the next round. Print each suggested need on the board. Call a new number each round.

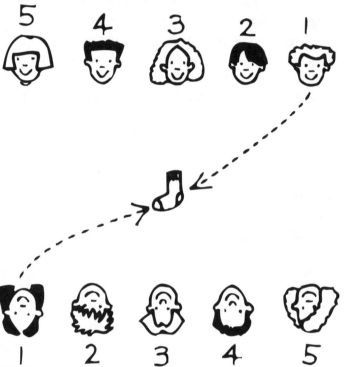

Options

1. If you have a wide variety of ages in the group, assign numbers so that students compete against kids of similar ages.

2. Play this game using objects which more closely represent needs students may have: water bottle, jacket, apple, book, photo of family or friends, and so forth.

Discussion Questions

1. **How is something you need different from something you want?**
2. Have a volunteer read Philippians 4:19 aloud. **How does God meet our needs?**
3. **In what way might God use you to meet another person's needs?**

Big Book of Bible Games
for Elementary Kids
© David C Cook. Permission granted to photocopy for ministry purposes only.

Partner Play

Bible Focus ▸ Matthew 28:16–20; Acts 1:1–11

Materials
tennis balls

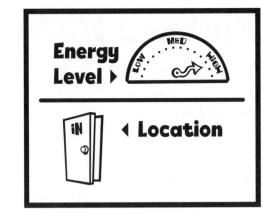

Lead the Game

1. **Because Jesus is alive, we know He will keep His promise to always be with us, helping us to obey His commands. Let's play a game in which we can win *only* by having a partner help us.**

2. Divide the group into equal teams of at least six students each. (If needed, you can join the fun!) Teams are to line up in single-file lines on one side of the playing area, leaving plenty of space between teams. Kids become partners with the team member behind them or in front of them in line.

3. Give the first partners in each line a tennis ball. At your signal, the first partners on each team should roll the ball back and forth to each other while moving to the opposite side of the playing area, then back to the line. The next partners repeat the same action. Keep playing until all the partners on each team have had a turn. Switch partners and play as time permits.

Options
1. If you have fewer than 12 students, partners could race against their own or other partners' times.
2. For a variation, partners could bounce a ball back and forth.

Discussion Questions
1. **What would happen if you had no partner for this game?** (I wouldn't be able to follow the rules of the game. I wouldn't be able to win the game.)
2. **Since Jesus is always with His followers, how can knowing that help you?**
3. **How does it make you feel to know that Jesus promises to always be with you?**

Picture Hunt

Bible Focus ▶ Acts 2

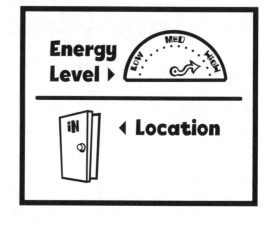

Energy Level ▶

Location ▶

Materials
old birthday cards, scissors, markers

Preparation
Cut the back off each card, leaving only the front design.

Lead the Game
1. **God gives us the Holy Spirit to guide us and to help us. When God first gave the Holy Spirit to Jesus' followers, the church began as a place where people could learn about Jesus! Let's play a game to celebrate the birthday of the church!**
2. Ask volunteers to suggest words, phrases, or sentences that describe the Holy Spirit (helper, teacher, guides us, sent from God, promised by Jesus). As sentences or phrases are suggested, print them on separate birthday cards. Make enough cards so there is a card for every two students. Repeat sentences or phrases as needed.
3. Ask kids to cut each card into two puzzle pieces.
4. Collect all the puzzle pieces and mix them up. Then distribute the pieces to students. At your signal, students race to match up their puzzle pieces. As kids match the pieces, they are to call out "Happy Birthday" and sit down. When all the pieces have been matched, the pair of students who sat down first can read the message on their puzzle pieces aloud. Collect the pieces and play again. Continue playing as time permits.

Options
1. Instead of using birthday cards, cut squares from birthday wrapping paper.
2. After cards have been cut into puzzle pieces, keep one piece of each card and hide the other piece in your room. Give each student one puzzle piece. At your signal, each student hunts to find the piece that fits his or her piece. After finding the piece, the student calls out, "Happy Birthday," then sits down.

Discussion Questions
1. **Why did God send the Holy Spirit?** (to help members of His family love and obey Him, to give us joy and hope, to be a deposit as we wait for heaven)
2. **What are some ways the Holy Spirit can help us?** (He will guide us in knowing the right things to do. He will remind us of God's commands and help us to follow them. He will help us know the words to say when we tell others about Jesus.)

Big Book of Bible Games for Elementary Kids
© David C Cook. Permission granted to photocopy for ministry purposes only.

Life Application Games

God's Love

God loves...

Action Relay

Bible Focus ▸ Psalm 105:2

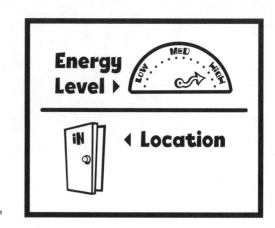

Energy Level ▸

◂ Location

Materials
Bibles, index cards, marker, paper bag (Optional: paper)

Preparation
Print each of these motions on separate index cards: skip, jump, tiptoe, walk backward, hop on one foot, slide, walk heel-to-toe, crawl. Put the index cards in a paper bag.

Lead the Game

1. **God's actions show His love for us. To celebrate His love for us, we're going to play a game in which we tell about God's loving actions!**

2. Group students into two equal teams. If needed, you can join the fun! Have the teams line up on one side of an open area in your room. Place the bag of prepared index cards on the other side of the open area.

3. **What is something recorded in the Bible God has done that shows the love He has for people?** (He sent Jesus to die for our sins, healed people, provided food and water for the Israelites in the desert, provided bread and fish for the people in Galilee.) (Optional: If students are not very familiar with Bible information, list responses on paper for use in the relay.) **To take a turn in our game today, you'll need to tell about one of God's loving actions!**

4. At your signal, the first student on each team runs to the other side of the room and says one of God's loving actions. Then the student moves to the bag of index cards and chooses a card. The student reads the card, returns it to the bag, and then returns to his or her team in the manner written on the card. Continue until all students have had a turn. Teams can sit down when all members have completed their turns. Ask the discussion questions below.

Discussion Questions

1. **When is a time a kid your age might experience God's loving care?** (when God answers a prayer, when God provides something my family needs)
2. **What are some good ways to learn more about God's loving actions?** (read the Bible, ask older people who love God about His loving actions)
3. **What can you do to tell others about God's loving actions?** Ask a volunteer to read Psalm 105:2 aloud.

Big Book of Bible Games for Elementary Kids
© David C Cook. Permission granted to photocopy for ministry purposes only.

Beat the Ball

Bible Focus ▶ 1 John 3:16

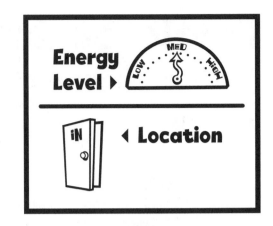

Materials
Bibles, foam ball (or tennis ball)

Lead the Game
1. Have a volunteer read 1 John 3:16 aloud. **We learn what love is like by looking at Jesus' life. Let's play a game to think about some of the different ways Jesus showed love!**
2. Ask kids to sit in a circle in the middle of the playing area.
3. Give the ball to a student. The student is to toss the ball to any other student in the group. As soon as the student tosses the ball, he or she gets up and begins running around the circle. The student who caught the ball passes it to the student next to him or her. Students quickly pass the ball around the circle, trying to get it back to the student who caught it before the runner returns to his or her seat.
4. The student who gets beaten (either the student who first tossed the ball or the student who first caught the ball) names one thing Jesus did to show love while He was here on earth. Keep playing the game as time allows, giving the ball to a different student to start each round. Between each round, ask one of the discussion questions below.

Options
1. If you have more than 15 students, form two groups to play the game.
2. As a challenge, older students can toss the ball to one another instead of passing it. Each student in the circle must still handle the ball as the runner returns to his or her seat.

Discussion Questions
1. **What are some ways Jesus showed love to people?** (He cared for people's needs, helped people get well, gave people food, was kind to people, and taught people about God.)
2. **When you are at school, what is one way that you can show love like Jesus did?** (forgive someone who is mean to me, be nice to kids whom others ignore)
3. **What might happen if we show love in some of the ways Jesus showed love?**

Footloose Relay

Bible Focus ▶ Genesis 1:26–28; 2:19–23

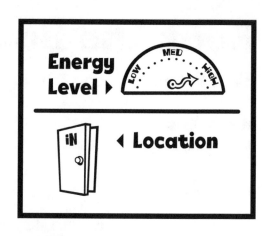

Materials
large length of roll paper, pencils

Lead the Game
1. **When God made the world and people, He showed His love for us. One of the ways He showed His love is that He created each of us a little differently. Let's find out one way each of us is special!**
2. Ask each student to trace a foot, with shoe on, on the paper.
3. Have kids line up across the room from the paper. (If you have more than ten students, have them form two or more teams and race against each other.)
4. At your signal, the first student(s) in line runs to the paper, finds his or her shoe outline, removes his or her shoe, and leaves it on the outline. The student returns to the line, hopping on the foot that still has a shoe on it. Kids in line repeat the process until everyone has had a turn.
5. If you have time, play another round, with each student tracing a hand. Each kid runs to the paper, finds his or her handprint, and writes his or her initials in it with a pencil. The student then skips back to the line. Students in line repeat the process until everyone has had a turn.

Option
If you have older students, play another round with students hopping back to the paper to retrieve each other's shoes.

Discussion Questions
1. **How did God make you the same as others? Different from others?**
2. **Would it be a good thing if everyone in our class was created exactly alike? Why or why not?**
3. **How did God show His love for us when He created everything?** (He made the sun so we would have heat and light and food. He gave us rain so we would have water to drink and that food would grow. He made each person with different abilities and interests.)

Full of God's Love

Bible Focus ▸ Acts 2; Romans 5:5

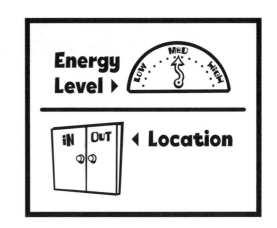

Energy Level ▸

Location ◂ iN OUT

Materials
for each team of 6 students: 2 containers (buckets, bowls, or plastic tubs), a small plastic cup, water, uncooked rice (or uncooked beans)

Preparation
Fill half of the containers with an equal amount of water and rice or beans. For each team, set an empty container and a full container next to each other on one side of the playing area.

Lead the Game
1. **Let's play a fun game to remind us of the Bible verse that tells us God poured out His love by sending the Holy Spirit.**
2. Group students into teams of no more than six students each. Teams should line up in single-file lines across the room from the containers. Give a cup to the first student in each line.
3. At your signal, the first student in each line runs to the filled container opposite from his or her team. The student uses the cup to take one full scoop, then pours the contents of the cup into the empty container. The student returns to the line and gives his or her cup to the next student, who repeats the process. Call out, "Full cups!" several times during the game. Each student with a cup in his or her hand when "Full cups" is called must go to another team's container and transfer a scoop for that team instead. The first team to transfer all its contents wins.

Option
Play the game outdoors and fill containers with a half cup of water. Give the first student in each team a straw. The student runs to the team's containers, puts the straw into water, and then places a finger over one end of the straw. Student then withdraws straw, positions it over the empty container, and takes his or her finger off the top of the straw to release water. The student runs back to the line and gives the straw to the next student in line.

Discussion Questions
1. **God has given us the Holy Spirit because He loves us. What are some other ways God has shown love to us?** (God sent Jesus to take the punishment for our sins. God created a beautiful world for us to enjoy. God answers our prayers.)
2. **The Holy Spirit helps us to show God's love and care to others. What are some things we can do for others with the help of the Holy Spirit?**

Human Bowling

Bible Focus ▸ Matthew 19:13–15; Mark 10:13–16; Luke 18:15–17; 1 John 3:1

Energy Level ▸ LOW MED HIGH

iN ◂ Location

Materials
Bibles, masking tape, rubber ball (or basketball)

Preparation
Use masking tape to mark a starting line.

Lead the Game
1. **You are important to God—and so is every person! Jesus showed His love for children when He told them to come to Him. Jesus' disciples tried to stop the children from seeing Jesus by sending them away. Let's play a game to remind us how much Jesus loves children and to remember that each of us is important to God!**
2. Select a volunteer to be the bowler. The remaining students— the human "bowling pins"—stand approximately ten feet away from the starting line in bowling-pin formation (see sketch). Students stand one arm's length apart (when arm is extended, student's fingertips touch a nearby student's shoulders).
3. The bowler names a way God shows love and rolls the ball, trying to hit the feet of one or more of the human bowling pins. The bowling pins must keep their left feet on the floor, but they may move their right feet to avoid being hit by the ball. The first student hit with the ball becomes the bowler for the next round. Continue the game as time permits.

Options
1. For groups larger than eight or nine students, form more than one game.
2. For each new round, the bowling pins switch positions, with students who were in the back moving to the front.

Discussion Questions
1. **How are important people usually treated?** (really well, driven around in special vehicles, others clap for them)
2. **How do we know we are important to God?** Ask a volunteer to read 1 John 3:1 aloud. (The Bible tells us we're important to God. We are called His children. God lavishes love on us.)
3. **What things does God do to show you are important to Him?** (He listens to and answers my prayers, sent Jesus to take the punishment for my sins so that I can live forever with God, and gives me people who love and care for me.)

Ladder Leap

Bible Focus ▶ Genesis 25:19–34; 27–33;
Psalm 136:1

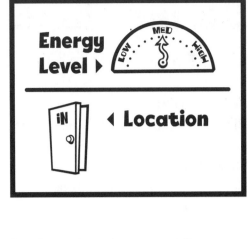

Materials
Bibles, masking tape, paper, marker

Preparation
1. Make a masking-tape ladder on the floor, with at least ten rungs or spaces (make one ladder for every ten students).
2. Print an action on separate sheets of paper, one for each ladder space: touch your toes, turn around three times, do five jumping jacks, shake hands with everyone in line, and so forth. Place papers next to each space, outside the ladder outline.

Lead the Game
1. **Jacob and Esau were two brothers who didn't always get along and spent many years apart. The two brothers had problems because of the many wrong things they had done to each other. But God helped the brothers to forgive each other and make peace. God loves us, even when we do wrong. Let's play a game to remind ourselves that God doesn't give up on us!**
2. Have kids form a single line. The first student hops on one foot through the ladder spaces while saying the sentence, "My name is (P-E-T-E-R) and God does not give up on me!" The student hops one space for each word and for each letter of his name. The student hops up and down the ladder as many times as needed to complete the sentence.
3. On the word *me*, the student stops and reads what the paper says in that space. Then the student leads the rest of the students in doing whatever action the paper says to do.
4. Repeat the game with each student in line.

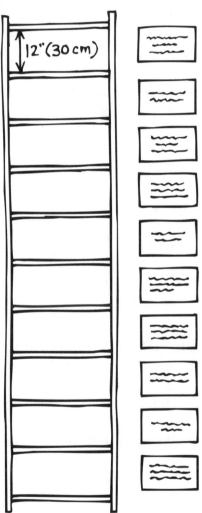

12"(30 cm)

Discussion Questions
1. **When might kids your age feel like God doesn't love them?**
2. **What should we do when we disobey God?** (ask God for forgiveness, ask for His help in doing right)
3. Have a volunteer read Psalm 136:1 aloud. **How do we know God will never give up loving us?** (God is good. God loves all people. God's love endures forever.)

String Hunt

Bible Focus ▶ Psalm 130:7

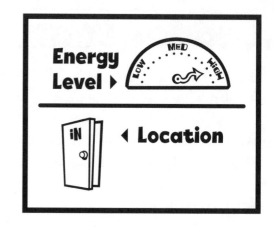

Materials
Bibles, string (or yarn), scissors, timer

Preparation
Cut string into varying lengths (at least two lengths per student). Hide string in the room.

Lead the Game
1. Have a volunteer read Psalm 130:7 aloud. **Let's play a game that reminds us of God's great love for us. In our game, the string we collect will get bigger and bigger to remind us that God's love is bigger than all the wrong things we have done.**
2. Group students in two or more teams of four or five students each.
3. At your signal, kids look for and collect the string pieces, trying to find as many pieces as they can in 30 seconds.
4. After time is called, team members are to lay end-to-end the pieces of string they've collected. The team that has collected the longest length wins. Continue playing the game as time permits.
5. At the end of the game time, tell the teams to use their strings to spell out *God's Love*.

GOD'S LOVE

Options
1. If space is limited, students could roll their strings into balls to see who collected the most string.
2. Depending on the number of kids in your class, vary the amount of time students have to collect the string.
3. To help students become better acquainted, form new teams for each round of the game.

Discussion Questions
1. **What are some big things that could remind you of how big God's love is?** (the ocean, a tall tree, a huge waterfall, the sky)
2. **How does God's love get rid of our sin?** (God loved us to much that He sent Jesus to earth. Jesus died on the cross to take the punishment for our sins.)
3. **What are some ways that Jesus showed God's love?** (Jesus made sick people well. He taught others about God. He died on the cross.)

Towel Travel

Bible Focus ▶ Mark 2:1–12; Psalm 109:26

Energy Level ▶ LOW MED HIGH

iN ◀ **Location**

Materials
Bibles; 2 each of these: towels, stuffed animals, balloons

Lead the Game
1. **A man who couldn't walk had four friends who were convinced Jesus could help their friend get better. So the friends carried the man on a mat all the way to the house where Jesus was.**
2. Have students form two teams. Teams are to line up in single-file lines on one side of the playing area. Give a towel and a stuffed animal to each team.
3. At your signal, the first four students on each team grasp the corners of the towel and place the stuffed animal in the center. Kids are to walk together, carrying the animal across the playing area and back. If the animal falls off, students are to return to the starting point and try again.
4. When the first group of kids is finished, the next four carriy the stuffed animal on the towel across the room and back. The relay continues until all students have had a turn. (Note: Some students may need to take more than one turn to provide a foursome for each turn.) Ask one of the discussion questions to a volunteer from the first team to finish.
5. **Now let's try to carry something a little bit harder! Give each team a balloon.** One student on each team should inflate the balloon. Have kids do the relay again, carrying a balloon on the towel instead of a stuffed animal.

Options
1. If some kids know the Bible story, invite them to tell other details about what happened.
2. If you have fewer than 20 students, they could work in pairs instead of foursomes to carry the towel.

Discussion Questions
1. **Jesus showed God's love as He healed the man who couldn't walk. In what ways can God's love help kids your age?** (God's love can help kids feel better about themselves. God's love can help kids who are going through a hard time.) Have a volunteer read Psalm 109:26 aloud.
2. **What are some of the ways sharing God's love can help people in your family? People at school? People in your neighborhood?**

Who Does God Love?

Bible Focus ▶ Acts 9:1–31; Romans 6:23

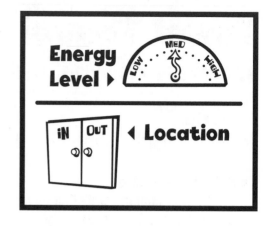

Energy Level ▶

iN OUT ◀ Location

Materials
blindfold

Lead the Game
1. **To become a Christian, we each must make a choice to accept God's grace and love to become a part of His family. The game we're going to play will remind us of God's love for us!**
2. Play a game like Marco Polo. Ask a volunteer to stand on one side of the playing area. Blindfold the volunteer. Students should quietly position themselves at random around the playing area. The volunteer begins saying, "God loves." The rest of the students should answer "me."
3. The blindfolded volunteer moves toward students by listening to their voices. As he or she continues calling "God loves," kids must respond each time. Depending on the size of your playing area, the students who respond to the blindfolded volunteer may stay frozen in one spot or may move around as they respond. (If you have a large playing area or a large number of students, kids should stay frozen.)
4. When the volunteer finds and tags a student, that student (or a student who hasn't had a turn yet) is blindfolded for the next round. Continue the game as time permits.

God loves...

Option
Instead of responding "me," students could respond with names of friends or family members.

Discussion Questions
1. **In the Bible story, what choices did Saul have to make?** (He had to choose to listen to Jesus. He had to choose to listen to Ananias. He had to choose to accept God's love and follow Jesus.)
2. **What is the most important choice anyone can ever make?** (to accept God's love and follow Jesus)

Big Book of Bible Games for Elementary Kids
© David C Cook. Permission granted to photocopy for ministry purposes only.

Life Application Games

God's Power

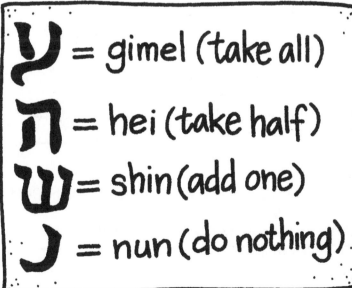

ג = gimel (take all)

ה = hei (take half)

ש = shin (add one)

נ = nun (do nothing)

Dreidel Power

Bible Focus ▸ 1 Kings 5–8

Energy Level ▸

iN ◂ Location

Materials

dreidels (1 for every 4 to 6 students), game pieces (at least 6 per student—small candies, nuts, paper squares, or pennies) (Optional: large sheet of paper, marker)

Lead the Game

1. **We can worship God for His great power and protection. In New Testament times, the Hebrew people worshipped God at the temple during a holiday called the Feast of Dedication, now called Hanukkah. This holiday reminds people of God's power. Let's play a game that is played by Jewish people today to celebrate Hanukkah.**

2. Divide the class into groups of four to six students. Give each group a dreidel and give each student at least six game pieces.

3. Have each group sit in a circle. Each student puts one game piece into the center of the circle. Students are to take turns spinning the dreidel and following the directions for the letter the dreidel lands on: *gimel* (GIH-mel)—take all pieces from the center; *hei* (HEH)—take half the pieces; *shin* (SHIHN)—add one; *nun* (NOON)—do nothing. (Optional: Print game instructions on paper and hang on wall for reference.) **The letters on the dreidel are the first letters from the Hebrew words for "a great miracle happened there." God's people believed God had done a miracle when, during the temple's rededication, a one-day supply of oil for the menorah lights lasted for eight days.** If all game pieces are taken, each student puts in one game piece. The game ends when one player has all the game pieces or when time is called.

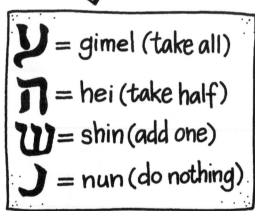

= gimel (take all)

= hei (take half)

= shin (add one)

= nun (do nothing)

Option

Play as part of a Hanukkah party. Decorate the room with blue and white streamers, play Hebrew songs, serve a holiday snack such as latkes (potato pancakes) or powdered donuts, and use chocolate foil-wrapped coins as game pieces for the dreidel game.

Discussion Questions

1. **What stories about God's power have you read in the Bible?** (parting of the Red Sea, Elijah being fed by ravens, Jesus healing a man who couldn't see)

2. **When have you been helped by God's power? How has God cared for you?**

3. **How do you need God's help and care today?**

Exodus Relay

Bible Focus ▸ Exodus 12

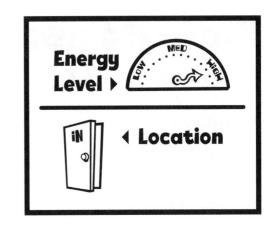

Energy Level ▸ LOW MED HIGH

IN ◂ **Location**

Materials
Bibles, 2 bathrobes with belts, 2 pairs of adult-size sandals, 2 walking sticks (or canes), 2 paper plates, crackers (matzos or saltines) Note: Be aware of food allergies or sensitivities and, as needed, provide alternatives for the crackers.

Preparation
On one side of the playing area, make two piles. Place one bathrobe, a pair of sandals, and a walking stick or cane in each pile. On the other side of the playing area, put a paper plate across from each pile and place half the crackers on each paper plate.

Lead the Game
1. **Whenever we need help, we can depend on God's power! That's what the Israelites did when they got ready to leave Egypt, where they had been slaves for many years. Let's play a relay game to remember what the Israelites did!**
2. **Guess where we're going to find the directions for today's game—in the Bible! Let's listen to the command God gave the Israelites when they were getting ready to leave Egypt.** Have a volunteer read Exodus 12:11 aloud. **For our relay, you're going to put on this cloak (bathrobe), put on the sandals, and carry the staff (cane) across the room to get a cracker from the plate. Then you eat the cracker and return to your team for the next player to have a turn.**
3. Divide the class into two teams. Each team is to line up by one pile of clothing. At your signal, kids should begin the relay. Continue playing until all students have had a turn.

Option
If you have more than 16 students, form additional teams and bring additional game supplies.

Discussion Questions
1. **When are some times kids your age need to trust in God's power?**
2. **When are some times God's power has helped you?** You may want to share your own answer before volunteers respond.
3. **What can we do to receive God's help?** (pray to God and ask for His help, read what God tells us to do in the Bible)

Slow-Motion Relay

Bible Focus ▸ Psalm 29:11

Energy Level ▸

iN ◂ Location

Materials

Bibles, masking tape, 2 chairs, children's music from your collection, music player

Preparation

Set up a relay course. Using masking tape, make a starting line on one side of the room, and place two chairs (or other objects) on the other side of the room for students to move around during the race.

Lead the Game

1. Divide the class into two equal groups. Each group should line up behind the masking-tape line for a relay race. At your signal, the first person in each line is to walk quickly to the other side of the room, around a chair, and back to tag the next person in line. Periodically, play a song. While the song is playing, kids must turn around and walk backward in slow motion.

2. The first team to finish the relay gets to answer the following question: **When is a time kids your age need to trust in God's power?** (when a family member is sick, when we need courage to tell the truth) Repeat the game as time permits.

3. After several rounds, ask the discussion questions.

Option

For variety, change the ways students move across the room while the music is playing (hop, crawl, tiptoe, and so forth).

Discussion Questions

1. **What does Psalm 29:11 say God does for His people?** Ask students to read the verse in their Bibles, and ask volunteers to give an answer in their own words.

2. **How might God give strength to one of His followers?** (God might give a person courage. God might send someone to help.)

3. **How do people who trust in God's power act when they are in difficult situations?** (They talk to God about the situation. They remember God's promise of help.)

Target Practice

Bible Focus ▸ John 9

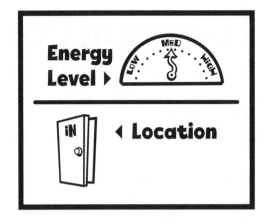

Energy Level ▸

◂ Location

Materials
large sheets of paper, markers, masking tape, index cards, scissors; 1 blindfold for every 8 students

Preparation
Draw several circles inside of each other on a large sheet of paper (see sketch), making one paper target for every eight students. Tape target(s) onto a wall at the eye level of students. Cut index cards in half.

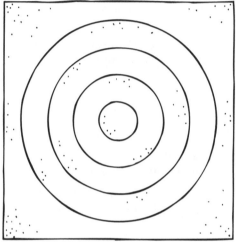

Lead the Game
1. **The Bible tells about Jesus healing a man who couldn't see. Let's play a game to find out what it might be like to be blind.**
2. Give each student half of an index card. Students are to draw a large X on the card and write their initials in one corner. Students should each make a masking-tape loop to put on the backs of their cards.
3. Play a game similar to Pin the Tail on the Donkey. Students are to stand in single-file lines of no more than eight students each, approximately five feet from a target. Blindfold the first student in each line. Each blindfolded student walks to the target and tries to put his or her X onto the center of the target. Then the student takes off the blindfold and goes to the end of the line. The next student in line is blindfolded and takes a turn. Repeat the activity until all kids have had a turn.

Options
1. If you are unable to use blindfolds, you could ask students to close their eyes while playing the game.
2. Assign points to each section of the target. Students take several turns each to see who can accumulate the most points.

Discussion Questions
1. **What are some ways we see God's power?** (when God answers prayers, when a person comes to know Jesus as Savior)
2. **What has God made that shows His power?** (storms, mountains, a beautiful sunset, powerful animals)
3. **In what ways can we worship Jesus for His power?** (sing songs about how great He is, tell Him what we love about Him when we pray to Him, thank Him for being our God)

Throwing Power

Bible Focus ▸ 1 Kings 17:7–16

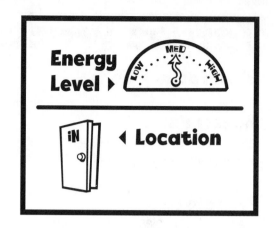

◂ **Location**

Materials
masking tape, cardboard box, timer, 2 colors of scrap paper

Preparation
Make two masking-tape lines 15' apart. Place the cardboard box in the center area (see sketch).

Lead the Game
1. **God's power was displayed when Elijah helped a poor widow have food to eat. Let's play a game about God's power!**
2. Divide the class into two equal teams. Each team is to sit behind a masking-tape line.
3. Give each team one color of paper (at least ten sheets for each kid on the team). At your signal, students begin making paper balls and throwing them into the box. Call time after 30 seconds.
4. One volunteer from each team collects the team's paper balls from the box and counts them. Another volunteer from each team collects the paper balls that landed outside the box and returns them to his or her team. Ask the team with the most paper balls in the box to tell one way that God shows His power by helping us in everyday situations. Keep playing the game as time permits. Be sure that both teams get to answer the question. Then ask the discussion questions.

15 feet (4.5 m)

Options
1. If you only have white scrap paper, mark each team's paper with a different-colored marker.
2. A laundry basket or other container can be used in place of a cardboard box.
3. To make the game harder, place the masking-tape lines farther apart.

Discussion Questions
1. **How do you see God's power in things He made?**
2. **What are some Bible stories you've heard about how God showed His power?**
3. **What kinds of problems might kids your age have? How might God show His power by helping with those problems?** (helping a kid to overcome a temptation to drink or take drugs, helping a kid to stop fighting with family members)

Life Application Games

God's Word

Drop and Freeze

Bible Focus ▶ Psalm 32:8; Acts 8:26–40

Energy Level ▶

◀ Location

Materials
children's music from your collection, music player, identical small object for each student (stackable block, plastic spoon, beanbag, eraser, etc.)

Lead the Game
1. **A disciple of Jesus named Philip helped a man understand the good news of Jesus from the words of the prophet Isaiah he was reading. Let's play a game to remember the good things that we can learn from the Bible.**
2. Divide the class into two teams. Identify the teams as team 1 and team 2. Give each student a small object. Let kids practice balancing the objects on their heads while walking around the room.
3. Tell students a way to move as they walk (heel-to-toe, tiptoe, baby steps, hop, and so forth). Play music as kids (hop) around the playing area, balancing the object on their heads. If the object falls off a student's head, the student immediately freezes and does not move until the music stops.
4. Stop the music after eight to ten seconds. Students with objects remaining on their heads when the music stops raise one or both hands (one hand if on team 1 or both hands if on team 2). Count the number of students with hands raised on each team. Ask the students on the team with the most raised hands to get together and tell some good news they have learned from God's Word. Continue playing as time allows. Alternate asking this question with one of the discussion questions.

Discussion Questions
1. **From the Bible, what good news have you learned about Jesus?** (Jesus died on the cross to pay for our sins. He rose from the dead. He healed and cared for many people.)
2. **From the Bible, what have you learned about God?** (God made the world and everything in it. God loves everyone. God sent Jesus to be our Savior.)
3. **From the Bible, what have you learned about how God wants His people to live?** (God wants us to be kind and patient. He wants us to love others. He wants us to share with others.)

Duck, Duck, Verse

Bible Focus ▸ John 3:36

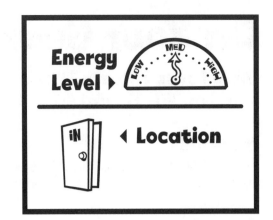

Materials
Bibles, index cards, marker

Preparation
Print the first sentence of John 3:36 on index cards, one word per card ("Whoever believes in the Son has eternal life.")

Lead the Game

1. Show students the cards you've prepared. **How would you put these words together to make a sentence?** Let students work together to make a sentence. Then ask students to turn in their Bibles to John 3:36, and have a volunteer read the verse aloud.

2. Play a game similar to Duck, Duck, Goose. Have kids sit in a circle, with one volunteer standing outside the circle. Distribute verse cards randomly to seated students. Students should place the cards faceup on the floor in front of them. The volunteer walks around the outside of the circle, lightly tapping each student on the head while saying the words of the first phrase of John 3:36 (one word each time he or she taps a person on the head).

3. When a volunteer comes to a student who has the same word that he or she is saying, the volunteer is to run around the circle while being chased by the student with the card. The volunteer tries to reach the empty seat before being tagged by the kid with the card. If the volunteer makes it, the kid with the card becomes the volunteer. Keep playing as time permits.

Discussion Questions
1. **How does a person come to believe in Jesus?** (reads the Bible, people teach him or her about Jesus)
2. **What will happen to people who don't believe in Jesus but reject Him?** (won't have eternal life in heaven)

On Your Guard

Bible Focus ▶ Psalm 119:11;
Matthew 4:1–11; Luke 4:1–13

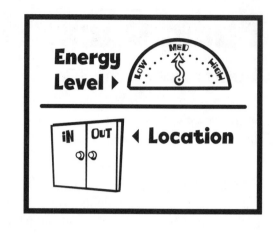

Materials
Bibles; masking tape; paper cups (1 per student); tape measure; at least 2 soccer balls, volleyballs, or tennis balls

Preparation
Divide the playing area in half with a masking-tape line.

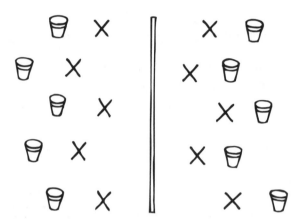

Lead the Game
1. **Knowing God's Word can protect and help us when we're tempted to do something wrong. In the game you're going to play, you're also going to protect something!**
2. Group students into two equal teams, one group on each side of the dividing line. Give each student a paper cup. Each student places the cup somewhere in his or her team's playing area, no more than 20' from the dividing line. Each students should stand about halfway between his or her cup and the dividing line.
3. Give a ball to one of the teams. A volunteer from that team rolls the ball across the dividing line, trying to knock down some of the other team's cups. The kids standing in front of their cups attempt to protect them, blocking the ball with their hands or feet. The student who catches the ball rolls it back across the center line toward the opposite team's cups. (Note: If no cups are knocked down after several minutes of play, add another ball or two so more than one ball is in play at the same time.) Call time after several minutes. Ask one or more of the discussion questions. Set up the cups again, and begin a new round of play.

Discussion Questions
1. Have a volunteer read Psalm 119:11 aloud. **What does the Bible tell us to do to protect ourselves from doing wrong or sinning?** (read and study God's Word, memorize God's Word)
2. **What wrong things are kids your age tempted to do? How can God's Word help and protect you when you're tempted to do something wrong?** (I can remember what God's Word says is the right thing to do, and then I can do the right thing.)
3. **In His Word, God promises to never leave His children. How can knowing this promise help you when you're tempted to do something wrong?** (I can remember that God is with me and will help me and give me courage to do the right thing.)

Picture-Puzzle Relay

Bible Focus ▸ Psalm 119:130; John 20:31

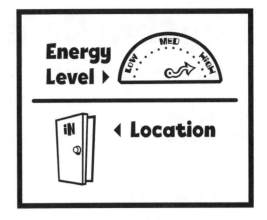

Energy Level ▸

Location

Materials
puzzles with about 12 pieces each (1 puzzle for every 6 to 8 students)

Lead the Game
1. **We put puzzles together to see the pictures they make. Reading the Bible is sort of like putting together a puzzle. All the stories we read in the Bible help us see a true picture of who God is so we can know Him and love Him!**
2. Divide the class into teams of six to eight students.
3. Ask the teams to form lines. Mix up the puzzle pieces and place them about 20 feet from the teams, keeping each team's puzzle pieces separate.
4. At your signal, the first student on each team runs to his or her team's puzzle pieces, gets a piece, and returns to the line. The student tags the next student to run to the puzzle and get a piece. Play continues until all the puzzle pieces have been collected. Then the kids on each team should work together to assemble their puzzle. Play additional rounds as time allows, trading puzzles each round.

Option
If puzzles are not available, print Psalm 119:30 or John 20:31 on index cards, one word per card. Play the relay as instructed above, substituting index cards for puzzle pieces and having teams put cards in correct verse order.

Discussion Questions
1. **What are some things you've learned from the Bible about God?** (He loves all people. He is more powerful than anyone. He is the only true God. He sent Jesus to be our Savior.)
2. **What are some of your favorite Bible stories?**

Rhythm Relay

Bible Focus ▸ 2 Timothy 3:16–17

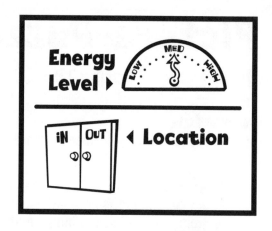

Energy Level ▸

iN OuT ◂ Location

Materials
Bibles, children's music from your collection, music player

Lead the Game
1. **When we know God's Word, it shows in our lives! Let's think about that as we play a game.**
2. Group students into at least two even-numbered teams. Have kids form pairs within teams.
3. Demonstrate a grapevine step, moving sideways by bringing the left foot in front of the right foot to take a step (see sketch) and then moving the right foot out to the right side to take the next step. Ask kids to practice the step in pairs, holding their arms over their partners' shoulders. After practicing, students should form teams again on one side of an open playing area.
4. Play music. At your signal, the first pair on each team takes grapevine steps to the opposite side of the playing area and back, tagging the next pair in line to repeat the action. When all the pairs on a team have had a turn, ask the winning team to answer one of the discussion questions. Continue the game as time permits.

Options
1. If you have space or can play this relay game outdoors, students could form pairs and all pairs race each other at the same time.
2. Students could do the steps as individuals rather than in pairs.
3. During the relay, you could play upbeat Hebrew music.

Discussion Questions
1. Have a volunteer read 2 Timothy 3:16–17 aloud. **What does it mean that Scripture is "God-breathed"?** (God inspired the writing of Scripture.)
2. **What do we learn from reading God's Word?** (how to love and obey God, how to show His love to others. How to become members of God's family.)
3. **Who has helped you learn from God's Word?**

Sheep's Tail

Bible Focus ▶ Joshua 23:14

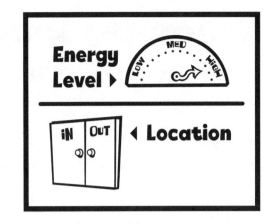

Materials
Bibles, fabric strips, ruler, scissors, masking tape, paper (Optional: rope)

Preparation
Cut one 2" x 10" fabric strip for each student. Using masking tape, mark off a large area of the classroom. (Optional: Mark boundaries of an outdoor playing area with rope.) Using small pieces of paper, mark some of the following verses in Bibles so students can quickly find them: Deuteronomy 31:8; Psalm 34:17; 100:5; Isaiah 41:10; Jeremiah 29:12; 31:3; 32:27; John 1:12; 14:23; Hebrews 13:8; 1 John 1:9; 5:14.

Lead the Game
1. Lead students in playing a game called Sheep's Tail. Using masking tape, attach fabric strips to the backs of kids' clothing. At your signal, students try to capture each other's tails (see sketch) while moving only within the boundaries, the "sheep pen." When a student's tail gets taken, he or she cheers for the others from outside the sheep pen until the next game begins.
2. The last student with his or her tail in place reads aloud a verse from one of the Bibles you've marked. **This verse tells about one of God's promises. What promise does this verse tell about?** Extend your discussion about God's promises by asking the discussion question. Continue the game as time allows.

Discussion Questions
1. Have a volunteer read Joshua 23:14. **What do you learn about God and His promises from this verse?**
2. **What does God promise when we ask for forgiveness?** (In 1 John 1:9, God promises to forgive us when we admit we've done wrong things.)
3. **How do God's promises encourage you?**

Treasure Hunt

Bible Focus ▶ Psalm 119:127;
Jeremiah 1:4–10; 36:1—40:16

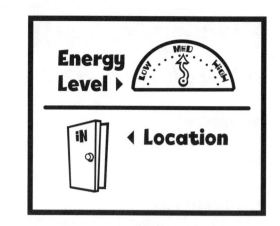

Energy
Level ▶ LOW MED HIGH

iN ◀ Location

Materials
Bibles, coins (at least 2 per student), small plastic bags

Preparation
Around the playing area, hide at least two coins for each student.

Lead the Game

1. **God's Word is so valuable because it tells us the best way to live. Let's go on a treasure hunt to remind us that God's Word is like a treasure!**
2. Have kids pair up. Tell each pair to come up with a signal that they will use to call each other (three claps, calling out a certain word, a whistle). Within each pair, one student will be the scout who looks for the treasure, and the other will be the collector. Give each collector a small plastic bag.
3. At your signal, the scouts move around the playing area to begin searching for the treasure (the coins you've hidden). When a scout finds a coin, he or she cannot touch it, but instead must use the signal to call the collector. When the collector hears the signal, he or she must go and pick up the treasure and put it in their plastic bag. Continue the game until each pair has located at least one coin.
4. Begin a new round of the game with kids trading roles. As needed, hide additional coins.

Options
1. Have students count their coins to determine the winning pair.
2. Substitute gold-wrapped chocolate coins for coins.

Discussion Questions
1. Ask a volunteer to read Psalm 119:127 aloud. **How is God's Word more valuable than money or gold?** (God's Word helps us get to know God and everything He has done for us. It tells us how to accept Jesus as our Savior.)
2. **How can we show our love for God's Word?** (pay attention to what it says, do our best to obey it, read it, study it)
3. **Who helps you learn about God's Word?**

Life Application Games

Holidays and Special Days

Candy-Heart Relay

Bible Focus ▶ 1 Corinthians 13:4

Energy Level ▶

iN ◀ Location

Materials

Bibles, disposable bowls, conversation candy hearts, plastic spoons, snack-size resealable plastic bags

Preparation

Place two empty bowls on one side of an open area in the classroom. On the other side of the room, place two bowls filled with equal amounts of candy.

Lead the Game

1. **God's love for us is the greatest love of all! On Valentine's Day, people talk a lot about love, send cards, and eat candy. But often, they forget about God and the love He has for us. Let's play a game with candy to celebrate God's love!**
2. Group students into two teams. Teams should line up by the empty bowls. Give the first student on each team a spoon.
3. At your signal, the first student on each team walks quickly to his or her team's bowl of candy and fills the spoon with candy. The student returns with the candy and dumps it into the team's empty bowl. If any candy is dropped, tell kids to leave it on the floor. (Be sure to throw away the candy that has dropped.) The next student in line repeats the action. Play continues until both teams have transferred all the candies from one bowl to the other. Have a volunteer from the first team finished answer one of the discussion questions. Keep playing as time permits.
4. Let students take home some candy hearts in plastic bags.

Option

If you have more than 12 students, form additional teams and provide additional materials.

Discussion Questions

1. **What are some ways God's love is different from the love people have for one another?** (God always loves us, no matter what. We don't have to do anything to earn God's love for us.)
2. Have a volunteer read 1 Corinthians 13:4–7 aloud. **How do these verses describe the kind of love God wants us to have for each other?**
3. **What are some ways we can show God's love to others?**

Christmas Hunt

Bible Focus ▶ Psalm 9:1; Luke 2:22–38

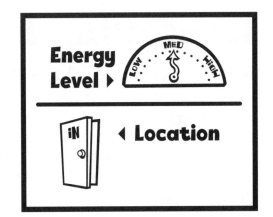

Energy Level ▶

LOW   MED   HIGH

iN   ◀ **Location**

Materials
Bibles, long length of roll paper, marker, small Christmas object (Christmas sticker on a small piece of paper, unbreakable ornament, or nativity figure)

Preparation
Print several prayer starters on the length of roll paper, such as: "Thank You, God, for …" and "Jesus, You are …" Leave space for kids to complete the prayers and write other sentences. Hide the Christmas object somewhere in the room.

Lead the Game
1. **There is a (Christmas sticker) hidden somewhere in the room. When you see it, quickly sit down in the center of the room without telling where the object is.** When two or three students have located the object and are seated, call the remaining students to also come to the center of the room. Ask the student who was the first one seated to retrieve the object. Review the story of Simeon and Anna by asking the discussion questions.
2. **One way we can show God we're thankful He sent Jesus to be our Savior is by telling Him in prayer.** Ask a volunteer to read Psalm 9:1 aloud. Show kids the paper with the prayer starters. Ask a volunteer to complete one of the prayer starters, praising Jesus for who He is or thanking God for sending Jesus.
3. Then have kids close their eyes while the student who wrote the prayer hides the Christmas object. Repeat the activity. Keep playing as time permits.
4. Close with a time of prayer, using the prayers that students have written.

Discussion Questions
1. **Who did Simeon and Anna find at the temple?** (the baby Jesus)
2. **Simeon prayed to God and said his eyes had seen the salvation God had prepared. Who was Simeon talking about?** (Jesus) **Why do you think Simeon said that?** (Simeon knew Jesus was the one who would save people from their sins.)
3. **What did Simeon and Anna do when they saw Jesus?** (They thanked and praised God. They told others about Jesus.)

Christmas Scrolls

Bible Focus ▶ Luke 2:1–20

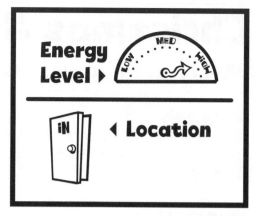

Energy Level ▶

Location

Materials

masking tape, 3 long lengths of roll paper, 2 lengths of yarn, 3" x 5" pieces of red and green construction paper, markers, 2 rolls of tape

Preparation

Make a masking-tape line on one side of your classroom. Roll up two of the lengths of roll paper to make two scrolls, and tie each with yarn.

Lead the Game

1. Invite students to list as many ways to celebrate Jesus' birth as they can (singing Christmas carols, decorating, making cookies, sending Christmas cards). List kids' ideas on one of the lengths of paper. Each student should write one idea from the list on a piece of red or green paper.

2. Divide the class into two teams. (Students are to keep their own pieces of paper.) Have teams line up behind the masking-tape line. Place one scroll and one roll of tape opposite each team on the other side of the room. At your signal, the first player on each team is to run with his or her piece of paper to his or her team's scroll and untie it. Players are to tape their papers to the scroll before rolling it back up. Continue until all players have completed the relay.

3. Ask two volunteers from the winning team to unroll the team's scroll and hold it open. Read aloud the ways of celebrating Jesus' birth attached to the scroll. Use the discussion questions to talk about the ways to celebrate Jesus' birth. Then ask two volunteers from the other team to do the same.

4. Invite students to write their initials on at least a couple ways that they plan to help others celebrate God's gift of Jesus.

Discussion Questions

1. **How does (singing Christmas carols) remind you of God's gift of Jesus?**
2. **How can this way of celebrating help you share with others the good news of Jesus' birth?**
3. **What are some other ways we can help others celebrate God's gift of Jesus?** (send a Christmas card about Jesus to someone who doesn't know about Him, invite a friend to come to a special Christmas event at church)

Christmas-Tree Relay

Bible Focus ▶ Luke 2:1–20

Energy Level ▶

◀ Location

Materials
colored paper cups

Lead the Game
1. **At Christmas, we worship God because He loved us so much He sent Jesus, the Savior. Some people celebrate Christmas by decorating Christmas trees. Let's play a game to build our own Christmas trees!**
2. Group students into teams of no more than six students each. Teams should line up in single-file lines on one side of the playing area. Give each team six cups.
3. Demonstrate how to stack cups to build a Christmas tree (see sketch). At your signal, the first student on each team runs to the opposite side of the playing area and sets down his or her cup. Then that player returns to his or her team and tags the next student in line. Team members repeat the same actions. Ask a discussion question to the first team that finishes building a Christmas tree. Mix up the teams and play again. Continue the game as time permits.

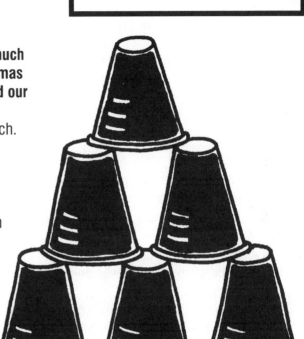

Options
1. Use cups with a Christmas design.
2. To make the relay more challenging, provide ten cups for each team. Print the letters of the sentence "Worship God" on paper cups, one letter on each cup. Team members complete the relay in the correct order to build a tree that spells "Worship God" from the top down.

Discussion Questions
1. **What fun things do you and your family do to celebrate Christmas?**
2. **What can we thank God for at Christmas?** (His love, sending Jesus as the Savior)
3. **How does giving and receiving gifts help us celebrate Jesus' birth?** (It can help us remember that Jesus is God's gift to us.)

Full of Life

Bible Focus ▸ Mark 16:1–7

Energy Level ▸

Location ◂

Materials
5 long lengths of roll paper, markers, masking tape, small slips of paper, paper bag, pencils

Preparation
On large lengths of paper, write one of these sentence starters:
"I can follow Jesus by …," "I'm glad Jesus is alive because …,"
"I want to praise God by …," "I thank God for His Son because …," "I will celebrate Jesus' resurrection by…."
Attach the papers to a wall, and place markers near the papers. On small slips of paper, print different ways to move, such as: crabwalk, skip, hop on one foot, walk backward, crawl, and so forth). Place the slips of paper in a paper bag.

Lead the Game
1. Distribute blank slips of paper and pencils to students. Ask kids to choose one of the sentence starters and to complete the sentence by either writing words or drawing pictures on their papers.
2. Ask kids to line up across from the papers on the wall. Tell the first student to choose a slip of paper from the bag, read it, then put it back in the bag. The student is to move in the manner written on the slip of paper to the paper on the wall that has the sentence starter on it that he or she completed. The student should write or draw his or her sentence completion on the paper and then continue moving in the same manner back to the line. Each student should do the same actions.
3. When all students have completed the activity, ask the discussion questions.

Discussion Questions
1. **Why is Jesus the only one who could take the punishment for our sins?** (Jesus is the only person who never sinned. Jesus is the only perfect sacrifice for our sins.)
2. **When we choose to become members of God's family, what does He give us?** (forgiveness of our sins, the Holy Spirit, eternal life)
3. **What are some ways we can remember Jesus' death and celebrate His resurrection?** (thank Jesus for dying on the cross for us, sing special songs about Jesus, celebrate Easter with our church families at special worship services)
4. **How does your family like to celebrate Jesus' resurrection?**

Journey to Bethlehem

Bible Focus ▸ Matthew 2:1–16; John 8:12

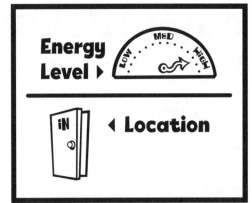

Energy Level ▸

iN ◂ Location

Materials
Bibles, roll paper, markers, tape measure, colored construction paper, beanbag

Preparation
Draw a 4' star on a length of roll paper. Draw lines to divide the star into five sections, and then label the star as shown in sketch a. Print "Bethlehem" on a sheet of construction paper.

Lead the Game
1. **We can worship Jesus as the Savior whom God sent for the whole world! Some of the first people who worshipped Jesus—the Magi—went on a long journey to find Jesus in Bethlehem. Let's play a game to take a journey to Bethlehem too!**
2. Give each student three or four sheets of construction paper. Tell kids to draw stars on each sheet of paper.
3. Ask students to place their star papers on the floor to form a game path. Place the star you prepared near the path, and place the Bethlehem paper at the end of the game path. Choose one student to be the helper.
4. Students should line up at the beginning of the game path. Students are to take turns tossing the beanbag onto the large star you prepared and moving the number of spaces written in the section that the beanbag landed in (see sketch b). As needed, the helper retrieves the beanbag and moves the large star around for students. (If a star paper is already occupied, the student moves to the next unoccupied star paper.) The first kid to reach the Bethlehem paper answers one of the discussion questions. Play the game again with a new helper.

Discussion Questions
1. **Why did the Magi want to worship Jesus?** (The Magi thought Jesus was the king of the Jews.) **What gifts did the Magi give to Jesus?** (gold, frankincense, myrrh)
2. **What is one thing that Jesus called himself?** (the Light of the World) Ask a student to read John 8:12 aloud.
3. **What gifts can we give to Jesus, the Light of the World?** (We can give our praise and worship. We can give our thanks. We can serve others. We can tell others about Jesus.)

Joyful Relay

Bible Focus ▸ Psalm 95:1; John 20

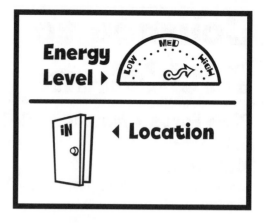

Energy Level ▸

Location

Materials
Bibles, index cards, marker, 2 paper bags, children's music from your collection, music player

Lead the Game
1. Have a volunteer read Psalm 95:1. **Knowing Jesus is alive gives us great joy! Let's play a game using some joyful actions to remind ourselves to celebrate.**
2. **What are some actions people do to show they are full of joy?** (smile, sing, jump, clap, cheer, high-five, skip) List each of the students' ideas on two separate index cards to create two identical sets of cards. Put one set of cards into each bag.
3. Group students into two equal teams. Teams should line up single file on one side of the playing area. Place a bag of cards across the playing area from each team.
4. Play some upbeat music. When the music begins, the first kid on each team runs to the paper bag and takes out an index card. The students read the actions and return the cards to the bags. Kids are to perform the action the entire time it takes them to return to their teams. The kids then tag the next students in line. Continue playing until each student has had a turn.

Option
If you have fewer than eight students, make one set of action cards and one set of directional cards (forward, backward, in a circle, sideways, by the table, etc.). Place each set of cards in a separate bag.
Tell kids to spread out around the playing area. While you play music, each student takes a turn choosing a card from each bag. The students hold up the cards so all the kids can see what's written on the cards and perform the actions as a group (for example, smile while moving in a circle). Continue until all students have had a turn choosing cards.

Discussion Questions
1. **What can you do to celebrate the fact that Jesus died for your sins and rose again?** (be happy about it, sing songs about it, thank Jesus for what He did for me, tell others about it)
2. **What can you do to share with others the joy that comes from knowing that Jesus is alive?** (I can tell others why I'm glad that Jesus is alive. I can invite my friends to come with me to church services. I can ask God to help me show joy to others and explain why I'm so glad.)

Palm-Branch Pass

Bible Focus ▸ Matthew 21:1–17; Mark 11:1–11; Luke 19:28–40; John 12:12–19

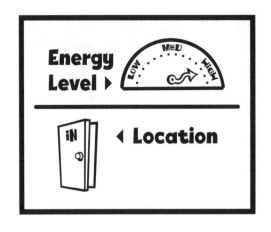

Energy Level ▸

Location ▸ iN

Materials
chairs (1 per student), small branch from a tree or bush for every 6 to 8 students, garden clippers

Preparation
Set the chairs in lines of four to eight, creating at least two lines of chairs as shown in the sketch. Trim off any sharp twigs from branches.

Lead the Game

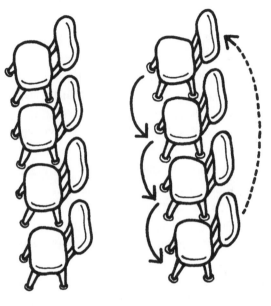

1. **We can't help but praise Jesus because of who He is and what He did for us! When Jesus entered Jerusalem the week before He died, people praised Him by waving palm branches in the air. Let's play a game with branches to remember a way Jesus was praised!**
2. Group students into teams of four to eight players. Assign each team a line of chairs, and ask students to sit down.
3. Give a branch to the student sitting in the first chair on each team. At your signal, the student passes the branch down the row. When the branch reaches the last student in the row, he or she holds the branch and runs to the first chair in the row. While the student is running, all the other team members move down one chair, leaving the first chair empty for the student who is running. After he or she is seated, the student passes the branch to the next student and the branch is passed down the row again. Continue in this manner until all kids have returned to their original chairs.
4. Ask a discussion question to a volunteer from the first team to finish the relay. Mix up the teams and play the game again.

Discussion Questions
1. **What are some of the reasons we should praise Jesus?** (He is God's Son. He was willing to die on the cross to pay the punishment for all our sins. He rose from the dead. He loves everyone. He taught us the best way to live.)
2. **What are some ways that we can praise Jesus?** (When we pray, we can tell Him why we love Him and what we're thankful for. We can sing praises to Jesus. We can worship Him.)
3. **What is your favorite way to praise Jesus?**

Palm-Branch Pickup

Bible Focus ▸ Matthew 21:1–17; Mark 11:1–11; Luke 19:28–40; John 12:12–19

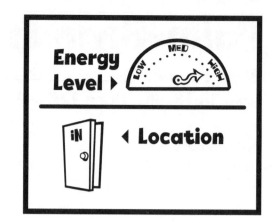

Materials
green construction paper, scissors (or paper cutter), markers

Preparation
Cut construction paper into small squares, making at least ten squares for each student.

Lead the Game
1. **When Jesus entered Jerusalem, people praised Him by covering the ground with branches from palm trees. Let's play a game and give praise to Jesus too!**
2. Give each student ten squares of paper and a marker. Students are to number their squares from one to ten and then randomly place squares, numbered side down, in the center of the playing area.
3. Divide the class into two teams. Teams should line up shoulder-to-shoulder on opposite sides of the playing area. Assign numbers to students as in the game Steal the Bacon (see sketch).
4. Call out two numbers. The kids from each team with those numbers have five seconds to collect as many green squares as possible. Call, "Stop!" when time is up. The kids return to their teams with the squares they collected. The team who collected the square with the highest number tells a reason to praise Jesus. If it's a tie, both teams tell a reason to praise Jesus.
5. Before playing another round, make sure all the squares are in the playing area, numbered side down. Play as many rounds as time allows.

Discussion Questions
1. **Instead of laying palm branches on the ground, how might we show praise today to an important person?** (have the person walk on a red carpet, clap for the person)
2. **What are some of the reasons Jesus is so great and worthy of our praise?** (He's God's only Son. Jesus took the punishment for our sins. It's through Jesus that we can have eternal life in heaven.)

Pumpkin Praise

Bible Focus ▶ Matthew 21:1–17; Mark 11:1–11; Luke 19:28–40; John 12:12–19

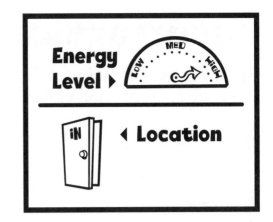

Materials
Bibles, 4 to 8 pumpkins of any size for every 10 students, black permanent markers

Preparation
In the playing area, arrange pumpkins to create an obstacle course (see sketch). Create one obstacle course for every ten students. Place a marker next to the last pumpkin in each course.

Lead the Game
1. **Thanksgiving time reminds us to give thanks to God! Let's play a game to thank God for the good things He has given us.**

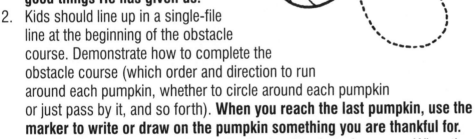

2. Kids should line up in a single-file line at the beginning of the obstacle course. Demonstrate how to complete the obstacle course (which order and direction to run around each pumpkin, whether to circle around each pumpkin or just pass by it, and so forth). **When you reach the last pumpkin, use the marker to write or draw on the pumpkin something you are thankful for.**

3. At your signal, the first student in line begins the obstacle course. When the student has finished the course and written on the pumpkin, he or she tags the next student in line, who begins the course. Continue until each student has had a turn. Then read all the responses that were written on the pumpkin, and let volunteers tell about the pictures they drew.

Discussion Questions
1. **What are some ways God cares for your family?**
2. **What is your favorite way to give your thanks to God?**

Resurrection Toss

Bible Focus ▸ Matthew 28; Mark 16; Luke 24; John 20

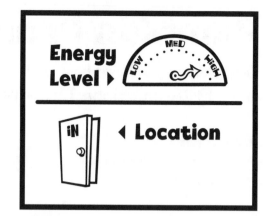

Energy Level ▸

iN   ◀ Location

Materials
paper plates, markers

Preparation
Print one letter from the sentence "Jesus is alive" on each paper plate. Use a different color marker for each set, and make one set for each team of students.

Lead the Game

1. **God's promise of salvation came true in Jesus' death and resurrection. Let's play a game that reminds us of Jesus' resurrection!**
2. Divide the class into teams of no more than 12 students. Each team is to line up single file at one side of the playing area. Give each student a paper plate written in his or her team's color. (If teams are small, some students can have more than one paper plate.)
3. Tell kids to take turns tossing the paper plates like Frisbees. Then, at your signal, the first student in each line runs to collect one of his or her team's paper plates. The next students in line repeats the process.
4. When all the paper plates have been collected, teams should put the plates in order to read "Jesus is alive."

Options

1. If you have a small playing area, challenge students to skip or hop (or another way of movement) to collect the plates and return to the line.
2. Have kids retrieve the plates in verse order.

Discussion Questions

1. **What are some other ways to complete this sentence: "Jesus is …"?**
2. **What are some ways we can thank Jesus for dying on the cross and taking the punishment for our sins?** (tell Him thanks when we pray, sing praise songs to Him)
3. **How does your family celebrate Jesus' resurrection?**

Ring Toss

Bible Focus ▸ Isaiah 9:1–7; Micah 5:2–4

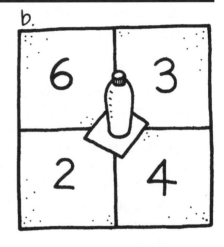

Energy Level ▸

◂ Location

Materials
paper plates, scissors, tape measure, stapler, roll paper, marker, small plastic water bottle filled with water, dry-erase markers

Preparation
Cut the center section out of two paper plates, leaving at least a 1"-wide ring. Staple the plates together, one on top of the other, to create a sturdy ring (see sketch a). On a 3' x 3' square of roll paper, draw and number the sections. Place the water bottle as shown in sketch b.

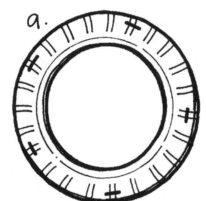

Lead the Game
1. **The prophets Isaiah and Micah told about God's promise to send a Savior. The season when people get ready to celebrate the birth of Jesus, the promised Savior, is called Advent. Let's play a game with things that will remind us of Advent and help us think about getting ready to celebrate Jesus' birthday.**
2. Ask students to line up approximately 4' from the prepared paper. Give the paper-plate ring to the first student in line.
3. At your signal, the first player tosses the ring at the bottle. The player gets the amount of points based on where the ring lands. (Note: A ring that circles the bottle scores ten points.) The player then retrieves the ring and gives it to the next student in line. The next player repeats the action. Let kids keep track of their points on the board. The student with the highest score when you call "Stop" is the winner. Then ask some discussion questions. Continue playing the game as time permits.

Discussion Questions
1. **What do you do to get ready for school? To go on a trip? To celebrate Christmas?**
2. **What do you and your family do to get ready to celebrate Christmas? Which of those things helps you to think about Jesus' birth?**
3. **How can you get ready to celebrate Jesus' birth?** (I can thank God that He sent Jesus. I can prepare gifts for others that help them think about Jesus' birth.)

Shepherd Relay

Bible Focus ▸ Luke 2:1–20; 1 John 4:9

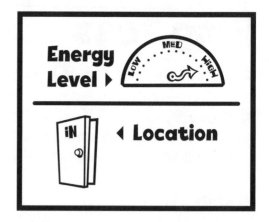

Materials
Bibles, a shepherd's costume (towel, bathrobe, sandals, walking stick) for each group of 6 to 8 students, large paper bags

Preparation
Place the costume for each group into a separate paper bag at one end of an open playing area.

Lead the Game
1. **The birth of Jesus the Savior is the reason the whole world can celebrate! Let's play a game as we dress up as the shepherds—the people who were the first to hear about Jesus' birth!**

2. Using the materials from one of the bags, demonstrate how to dress as a shepherd. When you are completely dressed as a shepherd, hold the walking stick and call out, "Jesus the Savior is born today!" Return materials to the bag.

3. Group kids into teams of no more than six to eight students. Ask the teams to stand in single-file lines across the playing area across from the paper bags. At your signal, the first student on each team runs to his or her team's bag, dresses up in the shepherd clothes, holds the walking stick, and calls out, "Jesus the Savior is born today!" The student takes off the clothes, puts them back in the bag and returns to his or her team. The next student in line repeats the action. Kids keep taking turns until everyone has had a turn. Ask a discussion question to the team that finishes first. Mix up the students, and play the game again.

Discussion Questions
1. **Why should everyone in the world celebrate Jesus' birth?** (Jesus came as the Savior for all people. God showed His love for the whole world when He sent Jesus.)
2. **What are some ways you, your family, or your church family tell others that Jesus was born?**
3. **How did God show His love for us?** Have a volunteer read 1 John 4:9 aloud.

Big Book of Bible Games
for Elementary Kids
© David C Cook. Permission granted to photocopy for ministry purposes only.

Life Application Games

Leadership

Hands-on Leaders

Bible Focus ▸ Old Testament Leaders

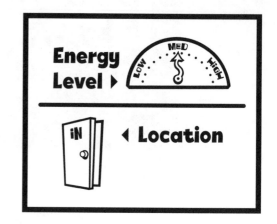

Energy Level ▸

◀ **Location**

Materials
roll paper, tape, marker, children's music from your collection, music player

Preparation
Cover a table with roll paper. Draw lines to divide the paper into sections, one section for each student. Print these Bible references in separate sections: 1 Samuel 10:1; 16:13; 1 Kings 17:2–4; 2 Kings 18:5; 2 Chronicles 5:1; 34:1–2; Nehemiah 8:2–3. Prepare one table for each group of seven students.

Lead the Game
1. **These Bible references tell about the people God chose as the leaders of His people. We can read true stories about what these people did in the books of History in the Old Testament part of the Bible.**
2. Students are to walk around the table while the music plays. When you stop the music, each student should put a hand on one of the sections of the paper. Each student is to turn in their Bible to the reference printed in his or her section. Invite students to read the verses aloud. Ask the discussion questions to explore the leaders.

Option
Provide several Bible dictionaries or let kids use online Bible dictionaries. Kids can find the names of leaders in the dictionaries and tell information about the leaders.

Discussion Questions
1. **What did this leader do?**
2. **How can the leader's example help you?**
3. **In what ways can you be a leader for God?** (be a good example for a younger brother or sister, commit to reading my Bible regularly, set a good example for others)

Leader Hunt

Bible Focus ▸ Old Testament Leaders

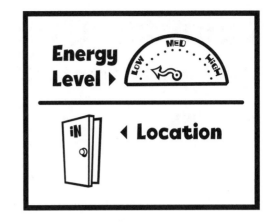

Energy Level ▸

◂ Location

iN

Materials
16 slips of paper, basket (or other container), pencils, roll paper (need a 3' paper square for each student)

Preparation
Number slips of paper from 1 to 16, and place them in the basket. Cut a 3' paper square for each student.

Lead the Game
1. **The first 17 books of the Bible tell us about the first people God made and the people who became leaders of God's people. Let's find and read about some of the people who were God's leaders.**
2. Each student folds a paper square in half four times, then unfolds the paper to reveal 16 squares. Kids should randomly number the squares from 1 to 16, writing the numbers in small print in the corners of the squares (see sketch).
3. Lead kids in playing a game similar to Bingo. Choose a number from the basket and read the number aloud, designating this square as the one to be used for the first round. Then say, **"Genesis 2:20."** Each student should read Genesis 2:20 in a Bible, identifying the name(s) of the Bible character(s) mentioned in the verse. Students are to write the name(s) of the Bible character(s) in the designated square. Continue the activity, choosing new numbers for the following references: Genesis 3:20; 6:8; 12:1; 21:3; 24:15; 25:25–26; 37:3; Exodus 2:10; Joshua 1:1; Judges 4:4; 6:12; 13:24; Ruth 1:16; 1 Samuel 3:10. After each Bible character is named, invite students to tell what they know about the leader. Play continues until a student has written names in four squares in a row.

Option
Repeat the game as time permits, having kids use the reverse sides of the paper squares or folding new papers.

Discussion Questions
1. **How would you describe this leader?**
2. **What things can we learn from this leader?** (how to love God more, how to stand up to negative pressure from friends, to make sure our words and actions match)
3. **What did this leader do that was good? Not good?**

Lead Me On

Bible Focus ▸ 2 Kings 6:8–23; 1 Timothy 4:12

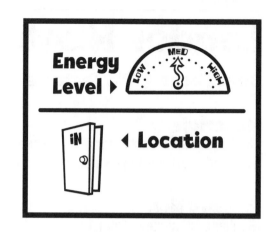

Energy Level ▸

◀ Location

Materials

Bibles, chair, table

Preparation

In the middle of the playing area, place a chair and a table where students can easily walk around them.

Lead the Game

1. **The prophet Elisha guided soldiers who were blind to the king of Israel, where the Lord opened their eyes. Elisha told the king to send the soldiers back to their country, and peace was restored between Israel and the surrounding peoples. When we do what's right, we can help others do good too. In the game we're going to play, your words and actions will help you to lead others on a safe path!**

Walk straight and then turn left.

2. Have three volunteers line up behind you and place their right hands on the shoulders of the students in front of them (see sketch). Tell volunteers to close their eyes. Give verbal directions for students to follow as you lead them on a walk around the room, between the chair and the table, and back to your starting position.
3. Repeat the activity, with a student acting as the leader and three to four students lined up behind the leader. Each time the activity is repeated, choose a different leader and rearrange the chair and table.

Options

1. Create additional obstacles: walk in and out of a doorway or walk a certain number of times around a chair.
2. If you have a large number of students, form several groups. Each group's leader guides his or her group on a different route around the room.

Discussion Questions

1. **How did the right actions of the leaders in this game help others?** (helped others walk safely around the obstacles)
2. **Whose good example have you followed? How might someone follow your good example?** (A younger brother might help someone who is hurt because I helped him when he was hurt.)
3. Have a volunteer read 1 Timothy 4:12 aloud. **How does this verse encourage you to be a leader, even though you are young?**

Line Leaders

Bible Focus ▶ Joshua 1

Materials
Bibles

Energy Level ▶ (LOW · MED · HIGH)

Location ◀ (iN OUT)

Lead the Game
1. **God helped Joshua get ready to lead the Israelites into the Promised Land. What did God do to help Joshua be a good leader?** (God gave instructions and promises to help Joshua.) **Today we're going to play a game in which we will need to be good leaders too!**
2. Lead students in playing a game similar to Follow the Leader. As shown in the sketch, have students stand in a single line. The first student in line is the leader. The leader stays in one place and begins doing motions (moves legs, moves arms, bends to the side, and so forth). The second student follows the leader; the third student follows the second; and so on (see sketch). There will be a ripple effect similar to the wave performed at a sporting event.
3. After several motions have been successfully completed, ask a volunteer to name something that God's Word teaches us to do. Ask the discussion questions to extend your discussion about the need to depend on God's Word to guide us. Choose a new leader and play the game again.

Options
1. Divide the group into two single-file lines with the line leaders facing each other. The leader of one line begins a motion, immediately followed by the leader of the other line.
2. Play the game outside and allow students to walk around as part of the motions.
3. If you have a large number of students, form several groups. Each group's leader guides his or her group on a different route around the room.

Discussion Questions
1. Have a volunteer read Joshua 1:6–9 aloud. **What are some of the instructions God gave Joshua? Which of these instructions can we follow today?**
2. **Who and what are some things kids your age depend on for guidance?** (parents, friends, teachers, Internet)
3. **When are some times you need God's Word to guide you?** (when a friend hurts my feelings, when I'm afraid, when I'm tempted to do wrong, when I feel lonely)

Loud Leaders

Bible Focus ▸ 2 Chronicles 34

Energy Level ▸

◂ Location

Materials
blindfolds

Lead the Game

1. **Even though Josiah was a young boy when he became king, he loved God. Good leaders do all they can to obey God and help others do what's right. Let's play a game to practice being good leaders for each other!**
2. Designate a playing area and help students get into pairs. Three pairs will play each round.
3. One student in each of the first three pairs puts on a blindfold. The partner of each blindfolded student takes off a shoe and places it somewhere in the playing area.
4. The shoeless partner and the blindfolded partner stand at the edge of the playing area. At your signal, the shoeless partner sends the blindfolded partner to find his or her shoe, giving directions such as, "Walk three small steps forward" or "Turn to your right and bend down." The student giving directions remains in place.
5. Once the blindfolded partner finds the correct shoe, the shoeless partner directs him or her back toward himself or herself. (Optional: The blindfolded partner must also put the shoe on the partner's foot.) Repeat play until all students have had a turn to be blindfolded.

Options
Make a separate playing area for each group of three pairs. Mark off the playing areas with masking tape, rope, or yarn.

Discussion Questions

1. **How was your partner a good leader? What would happen if you didn't follow your partner's directions?**
2. **Would you rather be a leader and help people know what to do or be a follower and do what a good leader says to do? Why?**
3. **How can people who love God be both good followers and good leaders?** (We can follow and obey God. We can help lead others to know God.)

Life Application Games

Obeying God

Balloon Challenge

Bible Focus ▸ Proverbs 3:3; Daniel 6

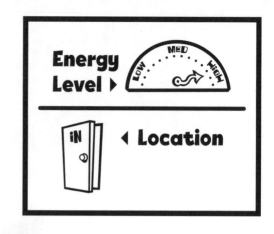

Energy Level ▸

◂ Location

Materials
balloons

Lead the Game

1. **Daniel had formed a habit of praying three times each day. When we form habits of faithfulness to God, it's easier to do what's right when trouble comes. We form habits when we practice doing something again and again until we can do it without even thinking about it. Let's practice this fun activity and see how good we can get at it!**

2. Help students form pairs. Give each pair a balloon. Tell kids to inflate and tie the balloons and practice hitting them back and forth to each other.

3. **Now that you've practiced hitting the balloon, count how many times you can hit the balloon back and forth before it touches the floor.** Have pairs continue the activity, challenging themselves to increase the number each time. **Imagine how much easier hitting the balloon would be if you had a habit of practicing it every day!**

Options

1. Students could vary the distance between themselves and their partners and try different hitting techniques to discover what works best for them.
2. You could challenge kids to use their heads, knees, or elbows instead of their hands to hit the balloon back and forth.

Discussion Questions

1. **What are some things kids your age try to get in the habit of doing?** (doing homework, brushing teeth, practicing a sport, playing an instrument)
2. **What kinds of habits could you form that would show your faithfulness to God?** (reading the Bible often, praying to God every day, doing what God wants me to do)
3. **How could developing these habits help you to stay close to God?**

Choice Moves

Bible Focus ▶ John 14:15

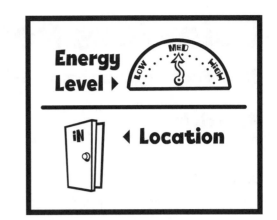

Energy Level ▶

Location ◀ iN

Materials
children's music from your collection, music player, 6 sheets of paper, 1 long length of roll paper, construction paper, markers, masking tape

Preparation
Print the letters C, H, O, I, C, and E on separate sheets of paper. Tape the papers to the floor in a large circle.

Lead the Game
1. **Jesus teaches that one way we show our love to God is when we obey Him. Let's play a game in which we tell ways we can obey God!**
2. Tell students to stand on or near one of the letters. (More than one student may stand on or near any of the letters.) As you play music, tell kids to move in any direction to new letters, making sure they are not standing next to the same students all the time. Stop the music. Call out one of the letters. The student(s) standing on or near that letter tells about a situation in which kids their age might find it difficult to make a right choice. Print a brief description of the choice on the large length of paper. Use the discussion questions to enhance the conversation. Repeat the activity until all students have had turns or all letters have been chosen.
3. You might want to tell students about a time you asked for God's help in making a right choice. Lead students in prayer, mentioning the choices on the list and asking for God's help in following Him.

Option
If you have fewer than six students in your class, students could walk around the circle as you play the music.

Discussion Questions
1. **What are some ways we can show we trust God when making choices?** (We can ask God for courage to do the right thing. We can remember His commands.)
2. **Which of these choices might be hard for you to make?**
3. **How can God help you when it's hard to obey Him and make the right choice?**

Coin-Toss Relay

Bible Focus ▶ 1 Samuel 15:1–26

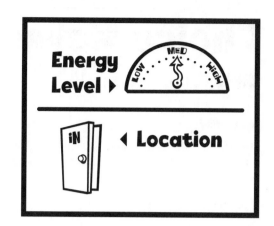

Materials
masking tape, coins

Preparation
Using masking tape, make two curvy paths on the floor in your playing area, leaving room for students to line up behind the paths.

Lead the Game
1. **God wants us to obey Him because He knows His commands are the best way to live. King Saul decided to follow his way rather than God's way, which led to God choosing a new king. We're going to do a coin-toss relay to remind us of the difference between choosing our own way and choosing God's way.**

2. Group students into two teams. Each team is to line up behind one of the masking-tape paths. **In this game, when your coin lands heads up, you'll get to move along the path in an easy way to remind you of how good it is to obey God's wise commands. If your coin lands tails up, you'll have to move along the path in a harder way to remind you that disobeying God causes trouble.**

3. The student at the front of each line flips a coin. If the coin lands heads up, tell the student to move along the masking-tape path in an easy manner (skipping or walking). If the coin lands tails up, tell the student to move along the path in a more difficult manner (crab-walking or putting one foot behind the other to move backwards).

4. After the first student has completed the path, the next kid in line flips the coin and moves along the path. Continue play until all students on one team have completed the path. If time allows, begin a new round of the relay with students doing new movements.

Discussion Questions
1. **What are some commands God wants us to obey?** (forgive others, love others, be kind and compassionate)
2. **What is a way that you can obey one of these commands?**
3. **What excuse might a kid your age give for not obeying God?** (it's too hard, no one else obeys God)

Connect the Part

Bible Focus ▸ Psalm 119:60

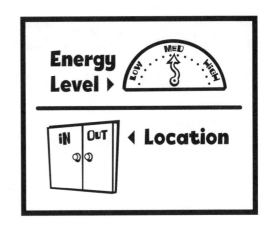

Energy Level ▸ LOW MED HIGH

iN OUT ◂ Location

Materials
index cards, marker

Preparation
Print the following words on index cards, one word per card: *elbow*, *foot*, *hand*, *shoulder*, *knee*, *back*, *wrist*, *toe*, *head*, and *finger*. Make one set of cards for every six students.

Lead the Game
1. **The words in Psalm 119:60 tell us it is good to obey God. Let's play a game in which we eagerly follow some funny commands to connect groups of people together.**
2. Group students into teams of six kids each. Distribute a set of cards to each team.
3. One student on each team acts as the cardholder. This student mixes up the cards and then holds them so that the other students can't see the words. Another student from the team picks a card and reads it aloud. Everyone on the team quickly connects the body part written on the card. (For example, the group stands in a circle with elbows connected in the middle.) The cardholder mixes up the cards and allows a different student to pick a card while the group stays in position. The group tries to connect by the new body part as well as keeping connected by the body part from the first card. When the group falls or can no longer stay connected, begin a new round with a new cardholder.

Option
If you have a small class, make one set of cards and have students form pairs. Choose two cards and read them aloud. Students in each pair connect the named body parts (such as wrist to ear). Mix up the cards and choose two new cards.

Discussion Questions
1. **What made it hard to stay connected? What made it hard to follow the commands?**
2. **In what ways can we learn about God's commands?** (read the Bible, listen to others teach from God's Word)
3. **When might a kid your age find it hard to obey God's commands?** (when I don't understand the command, when no one else seems to be following it)

Follow the Guide

Bible Focus ▸ Genesis 12:1–9; Jeremiah 17:7

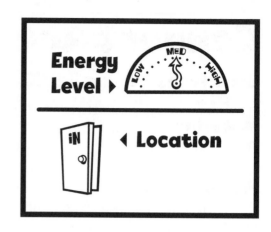

Energy Level ▸

◂ **Location**

Materials
Bibles, large sheets of paper in 3 or 4 colors, masking tape

Preparation
Around an open playing area, tape the sheets of paper to different walls.

Lead the Game
1. **Abram followed God's guidance as he left his home and went to a new place God showed him. God has also promised to guide and protect us, and we can always trust God's promises! Let's play a game in which you need to listen to a guide to succeed.**
2. **Listen carefully to what I say as your guide and follow my instructions.** Tell kids to begin walking around the playing area. Call out a number between two and four and instruct students to quickly gather in groups of that number, linking arms. Call out a manner of moving (hopping on one foot, skipping, tiptoeing, giant steps, baby steps). Groups should move in this manner, keeping arms linked. Then call out a color of one of the sheets of paper. Groups are to move quickly to the closest paper of that color, keeping arms linked and moving in the manner called. As each group gets to the paper, each member of the group must touch the paper. Then that group should sit down.
3. When all the groups have reached the paper, ask a volunteer from the first group to be seated to tell about a time when he or she trusted God's promise to guide and protect him or her. If the volunteer can't think of anything, he or she could name one of God's promises or repeat Jeremiah 17:7. Continue playing as time allows, varying the instructions for each round of play.

Discussion Questions
1. **How do your parents or teachers give you guidance or instruction?** (tell me what to do, show me how to do things)
2. **In what ways does God guide us?** (by His instructions in the Bible, by giving us people who tell us the right ways to love God and others, by answering our prayers)
3. **What are some ways to show that we trust God to be our guide?** (ask for His help when making choices, read God's Word to discover His commands)

Big Book of Bible Games
for Elementary Kids
© David C Cook. Permission granted to photocopy for ministry purposes only.

"Here I Am!"

Bible Focus ▶ 1 Samuel 3

Materials
blindfold

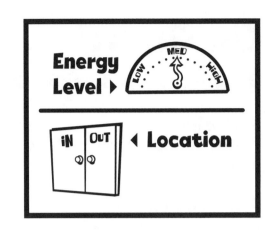

Energy Level ▶

Location ▶
iN OUT

Lead the Game
1. **Samuel was a man who listened to God his whole life. We're going to play a game that shows how important listening is.**
2. Lead kids in playing a game similar to Marco Polo. Ask a volunteer to stand on one side of the playing area. Blindfold the volunteer. Students quietly position themselves at random around the playing area. The volunteer begins calling, "Samuel, Samuel." The rest of the students answer with the phrase, "Here I am."
3. The blindfolded volunteer moves toward students by listening to their voices. As he or she continues calling, "Samuel, Samuel," students around the room must respond each time. Depending on the size of your playing area, the kids who respond to the blindfolded volunteer may stay frozen in one spot or may move around as they respond. (If you have a large playing area or a large number of students, kids should stay frozen.)
4. When the volunteer finds and tags a student, that student (or a student who hasn't had a turn yet) is blindfolded for the next round. Continue the game as time permits.

Option
You can play the game outdoors. Make the boundaries of the game area larger for an additional challenge.

Discussion Questions
1. **What are some ways we can listen to God and find out what He wants us to do?** (read the Bible, listen to adults who teach from God's Word, pray, talk with adults who know and love God)
2. **What do you think a person is like who listens to and obeys God?** (kind and patient, honest, obedient to parents, a good friend to others)
3. **What's one way that you have recently listened to God?**

On Guard

Bible Focus ▸ Judges 16:4–22

Materials

masking tape, tape measure, cardboard box, scrap paper in 2 or 3 different colors

Preparation

Use masking tape to make a 5' square in the middle of the playing area. Place the box in the middle of the masking-tape square.

Lead the Game

1. **Samson made some bad choices when he was tempted. God's Word tells us to be on our guard so we won't make bad choices when we're tempted to do something wrong. We can ask God for self-control to help us always make the best choice. Let's practice being on our guard in this game!**
2. Have kids form two or three teams. Have the teams stand on different sides of the playing area. Give each team one color of scrap paper. Students should wad their papers into balls. Choose one volunteer from each team to be a guard. Guards stand inside the masking-tape square in front of any team except their own.
3. At your signal, students attempt to throw their paper balls past the guard and into the box, making sure to stay behind the masking-tape line at all times. The guards try to block the paper balls.
4. After a short time, signal students to stop throwing the paper balls. Ask another volunteer from each team to collect their team's paper balls from the box, counting how many are in it. Then ask the team with the most balls in the box to answer one of the discussion questions. Keep playing as time permits.

Discussion Questions

1. **When might you find it hard to show self-control and need to remember to be on guard? Why?**
2. **Not having self-control and not being on your guard when you're in situations that may tempt you might get you into trouble. What might happen if you don't have self-control when you are tempted to (copy someone's homework)?**
3. **What kinds of good choices could you make when you depend on God for self-control?** (I can control my temper. I can obey God's Word by treating others kindly and not lying or stealing.)

Pharaoh, Pharaoh

Bible Focus ▶ Exodus 8–11

Energy Level ▶ LOW MED HIGH

IN ◀ **Location**

Materials
masking tape (or chairs)

Preparation
Use masking tape or chairs to mark a "safe" area.

Lead the Game

1. **Moses kept going to Pharaoh to ask him to let the Israelites leave Egypt. It was hard to keep asking Pharaoh, but God helped Moses. Let's play a game to act out what happened.**

2. Choose a volunteer to be Pharaoh. The rest of the kids will act as Moses and the Israelites.

3. Explain where the safe area is. Pharaoh should begin by walking outside of the safe area. Kids should follow him or her and ask in unison, "Pharaoh, Pharaoh, can we go?" If Pharaoh answers "No," students continue following and keep repeating the question. If Pharaoh answers "Yes," Pharaoh turns and chases the students back to the safe area. The first student Pharaoh tags becomes Pharaoh for the next round of play. If all students reach the safe area before they are tagged by Pharaoh, Pharaoh continues in his or her position or a new volunteer is chosen.

Discussion Questions

1. **What are some things kids your age do to love and obey God?** (be patient and kind, help an older neighbor, obey parents, be friends with a kid who is lonely)

2. **When might it be hard for a kid your age to love and obey God?** (when it seems like no one else is loving and obeying God, when I'm afraid of what my friends might think about what I'm doing)

3. **How might God help someone your age do what's right?** (He might give me courage. He might help me remember why it's the right thing to do. He might give me a friend who will do the right thing with me.)

Scrabble Scramble

Bible Focus ▶ Psalm 119:11

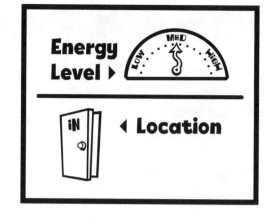

Energy Level ▶

◀ Location

Materials

Bibles, index cards, marker, large sheet of paper

Preparation

On index cards, print eight to ten key words about ways to remember God's Word, one letter on each card (memorize, sing, read, think, talk, draw, write, posters, friends, parents). Also list the words on the large sheet of paper and display it on a wall. Make one set of cards for up to 12 students. Mix up the cards, and spread them facedown at one end of the room.

Lead the Game

1. Ask students to find and read Psalm 119:11 in their Bibles. **How many different ways can you think of hiding God's Word in your heart?** (memorize Bible verses, sing verses, read the Bible, think and talk about what God says, look at posters that tell things the Bible says). **When you hide God's Word in your heart, it will help you when you're tempted to disobey God.** Divide the class into four groups. Distribute three blank cards to each group. At your signal, one student from each group runs to the card pile, takes seven cards, and returns to his or her group.

2. Then tell the groups to play a game of Scrabble together, taking turns spelling out words on the floor and connecting them as shown in the sketch. (If kids need help with spelling, remind them that they can look at the paper on the wall.) Students may use blank cards as "wild cards," substituting them for missing letters. As each word is formed, ask a volunteer to use the word in a sentence describing a way to learn about and remember God's instructions.

3. If a group cannot spell a word, it sends a runner to the card pile to take another card. Continue until a word can be formed. (If all the cards have been taken from the pile, the group loses its turn.) The game ends when one group has played all its cards or when no group is able to form additional words. Words may only be used once.

Discussion Questions

1. Read Psalm 119:11. **What does it mean to hide God's Word in your heart?**
2. **How can learning and memorizing God's Word help you make right choices?** (I can remember what God wants me to do.)
3. **When are some times it would help you to know a Bible verse to help you make right choices?**

Shuffle Feet

Bible Focus ▸ Daniel 1; Acts 5:29

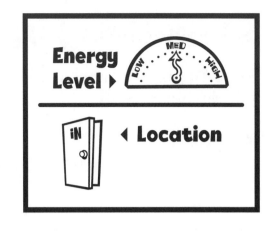

Energy Level ▸

◂ Location

Materials
Bibles, index cards, marker, 2 paper bags, 4 large tissue boxes (or empty shoeboxes)

Preparation
Print the following commands on separate index cards: Do three jumping jacks; smile and say hello to your teacher; clap seven times; wink at your team; turn around twice. Make two sets of cards. Place one set in each bag.

Lead the Game

1. **Daniel chose to obey God by refusing to eat the king's food that was sacrificed to idols. One way we can show love for God is by choosing to obey Him, even when it's hard. Let's play a game to obey some instructions, even if they are hard to do!**
2. Divide the group into two teams. Teams should line up on one side of the playing area. Place one bag of index cards on the opposite side of the playing area from each team.
3. Give the first student on each team two boxes. At your signal, the first student on each team steps into his or her boxes and shuffles to his or her team's bag. The students take out an index card, reads the command on it, and returns it to the bag. Then the student performs the action on the card, stepping out of the boxes as necessary. The student then steps back into the boxes, shuffles back to his or her team, and steps out of the boxes for the next student to begin the relay. The game continues until all students have had a turn.

Discussion Questions
1. **What was hard about this relay?** (moving quickly, completing a command with the boxes on our feet)
2. **What are some of God's commands from the Bible?** (love others, don't lie, don't worry) **When are some times it's hard to obey God's commands?** (when everyone else is disobeying God's commands, when I don't feel like being kind or loving)
3. Have a volunteer read Acts 5:29 aloud. **Why is important to obey God?** (His laws are the best, even when they are hard. He loves us. He is God, the maker of everything. His laws tell us how to follow His plans.)

Standing Firm

Bible Focus ▶ Nehemiah 1:1—8:12;
1 Corinthians 15:58

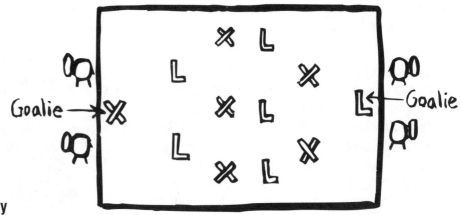

Energy Level ▶

◀ Location

Materials
Bibles, masking tape, chairs, tennis ball (or soft foam ball)

Preparation
Tear off masking-tape strips (two for each student). Position chairs as shown in the sketch.

Lead the Game
1. **Nehemiah led the rebuilding of Jerusalem's wall, even when others tried to stop him. God's Word tells us to patiently continue to do what is right in all situations. One way the Bible describes this is by telling us to stand firm. We're going to practice standing firm as we play a game of human foosball!**
2. Divide the group into two teams. Position students as shown in the sketch, with each team facing away from its respective goalie. Students should stand at least an arm's length from each other. Give each student two strips of masking tape. Ask the kids on one team to make masking-tape Xs on the floor to mark their positions. Students on the other team should make masking-tape Ls on the floor.
3. Gently roll the ball toward the middle of the playing area. Students are to try to kick the ball toward their team's goal, each student keeping at least one foot on his or her masking-tape mark at all times and not touching the ball with his or her hands.
4. Students should continue kicking the ball until a goal is scored. (Note: Goalies can only use their feet to defend their goals.) After each goal, ask the team that scored to answer a discussion question. Begin again by giving the ball to a player from the team that did not score.

Discussion Questions
1. **During this game, you stood firm by not moving off the tape. Listen to what the Bible says about standing firm.** Ask a volunteer to read 1 Corinthians 15:58 aloud. **What does it mean to "stand firm" and "let nothing move you"?** (keep on doing what's right no matter what, don't let others influence me to do wrong things)
2. **What is "the work of the Lord"?** (loving others, obeying God's commands)
3. **Name a time (at school) when it's hard to do what's right. How can you patiently keep doing right in that situation?** Repeat the question, substituting other places or situations.

Target Relay

Bible Focus ▸ Esther; Galatians 6:10

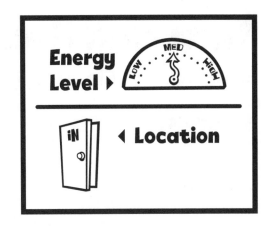

Energy Level ▸

Location ◂ iN

Materials
masking tape (or yarn), several Frisbees

Preparation
For every four to six students, make a 2' masking-tape or yarn square on one side of the playing area.

Lead the Game
1. **Queen Esther used the opportunity she was given to save God's people from destruction. We can please God by using every opportunity we have to do what is right. Let's practice doing what's right in our game!**
2. Divide the class into teams of four to six kids. Teams should line up across the playing area from the targets. Give the first person on each team a Frisbee. **For each round of the game, we'll have a different way to "do what's right," to correctly get the Frisbee onto the target. The first way is to hang the Frisbee by its rim on your fingertip and toss it onto the target.** Demonstrate the motion.
3. At your signal, the first student on each team hangs the Frisbee by its rim on his or her fingertip, runs across the room, and tosses the Frisbee onto the team's target. Whether or not the Frisbee lands on the target, the student retrieves the Frisbee and runs back to the line. The next student in line repeats the action.
4. When all students have completed the relay, announce a new way of "doing right," getting the Frisbee onto the target, and begin the game again. (Examples: rolling the Frisbee onto the target, tossing the Frisbee from a standing position, tossing the Frisbee back over the shoulder, rolling the Frisbee between the legs). Continue as time allows.

Discussion Questions
1. **What are some ways to learn what's right to do?** (read the Bible, listen to parents and teachers, watch older people who love Jesus)
2. **What are some ways that you can do good to others at school? At church? In your neighborhood?**
3. **What are some ways that you can remember to do what's right when you have the opportunity?** (pray and ask God to help you remember, think of a slogan or a question to ask yourself when you have a choice to make)

Turn and Run

Bible Focus ▸ 2 Chronicles 7:14; John 21:15–19

Materials
Bibles

Lead the Game

1. Have a volunteer read John 21:15–19 aloud. **Three times, Peter denied he knew Jesus. But Jesus forgave him, and Peter became a great leader of the early church. When we do wrong things, it's like turning away from God. But God offers to forgive us, and He wants us to turn back to Him. Let's play a game that reminds us of turning around to move in a new direction!**

2. Ask kids to stand shoulder-to-shoulder on one side of a playing area that's at least 40' long. Stand at the other end of the playing area and call out, "Run!" Students are to run toward you. Call out, "Freeze!" Students are to freeze. Then call out, "Turn around." The students are to turn away from you. Call out, "Run." Students are to run in the opposite direction from you. Continue calling out any variation of these commands (slow motion, crawl, hop, and so forth). The first student who reaches you becomes the caller and a new round begins.

Options

1. Blow a whistle before you call out each command so students know to prepare for a change.
2. If you have a smaller playing area than suggested, students may walk, crawl, or hop rather than run.

Discussion Questions

1. **When are some times kids your age might disobey God?**
2. Read 2 Chronicles 7:14 aloud. **What does God promise to do when we ask Him to forgive us?**
3. **When was a time that you decided you wanted to stop doing wrong things and, instead, asked God for help in obeying His commands?** You might want to give an age-appropriate example from your own life.

Two-by-Two Relay

Bible Focus ▶ Genesis 6:9—9:17

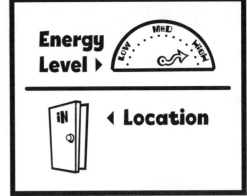

Energy Level ▶

◀ **Location**

Materials
index cards, marker

Lead the Game

1. **Noah showed his love for God by obeying Him and building the ark. We might even say the animals obeyed by getting on board! Let's play a game about the animals getting on board the ark!**

2. **What animals were on the ark with Noah?** Write on separate index cards the name of each animal students suggest. (You might want to prepare cards ahead of time.) Mix up the order of cards and place them in a stack.

3. **Many of the animals that came onto the ark came in pairs.** Ask kids to line up in pairs. (If you have an uneven number of students, form one or more trios.) Each pair of students takes a card and quickly decides an action to imitate the animal named on the card. At your signal, each pair is to link arms and move across the playing area in the manner chosen. When they get to the other side of the playing area, each pair should stand up and make the noise of their animal, then return to the line in the same manner.

4. If you have time, shuffle the cards and play again so each student gets a chance to imitate more than one kind of animal. Students could change partners for each round of the game.

Discussion Questions

1. **What animal would you most like to be? Why?**
2. **What animal did you have the most fun acting like?**
3. **Noah obeyed God by building an ark. What are some ways a kid your age can obey God?** (obey parents, love God, tell the truth)

Whisk-Broom Relay

Bible Focus ▸ Joshua 3

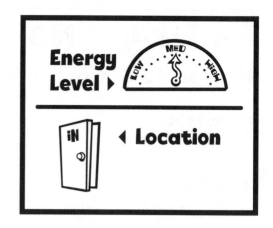

Energy Level ▸ LOW MED HIGH

iN ◂ Location

Materials

masking tape, items for obstacle course (table, chairs, books, etc.), balloons, 2 whisk brooms

Preparation

Lay masking-tape lines at opposite ends of the playing area. Use tables, chairs, stacks of books, or other objects to create two identical obstacle courses (see sketch). Blow up and tie two balloons.

Lead the Game

1. **Joshua obeyed God as he led the Israelites across the Jordan River. In our game, you'll guide balloons through an obstacle course!**
2. Divide the class into two teams. Teams are to line up behind the masking-tape line. Give the first student in each line a whisk broom and a balloon. Demonstrate the proper path through each obstacle course.
3. Students are to use whisk brooms to move the balloons through the obstacle course and back to the starting line, touching the balloons only with the brooms. After each student completes the course, he or she hands the whisk broom and balloon to the next student who repeats the course. Continue until all students have had a turn.
4. Ask a discussion question to the first team to complete the course. Repeat the relay as time allows.

Option

If space is limited, prepare one obstacle course and then time how long it takes each team to complete it.

Game Tip

In case balloons pop during the game, have a few extra balloons inflated.

Discussion Questions

1. **You encouraged your teammates to try to win the game. Who could encourage you to obey God?** (parents, friends, teachers)
2. **How could you encourage a friend to obey God?** (by reminding my friend how important it is to obey God, by helping my friend do something that's hard)

Life Application Games

Praising God

Leaven Hunt

Bible Focus ▸ Exodus 12:12–42

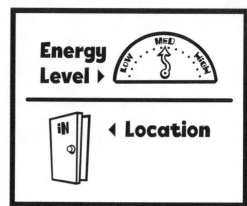

◂ **Location**

Materials

scissors (or paper cutter), construction paper in 2 colors, ruler, pencil, timer

Preparation

Cut construction paper into 1" squares, making approximately 40 squares of each color. Hide the squares in your room.

Lead the Game

1. **Every day we see things that remind us to praise God for the great things He has done! During the Passover celebration, Jewish people remember the way God rescued them from slavery in Egypt. Today we're going to play a game that reminds us how fast the Israelites left Egypt.**

2. **The Israelite people were to leave Egypt in such a hurry that God told them to make their bread without yeast, because it wouldn't have time to rise. Another name for yeast is leaven. The yeast or leaven is what makes bread rise or get bigger. To get ready to celebrate Passover, it's a custom to look all over the house to remove anything made with leaven.** Divide the class into two teams, and explain that each team will have 30 seconds to collect paper squares representing leaven. Assign each team one of the two colors.

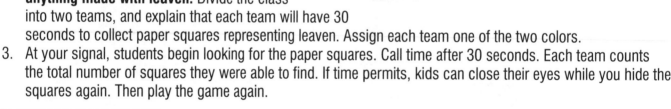

3. At your signal, students begin looking for the paper squares. Call time after 30 seconds. Each team counts the total number of squares they were able to find. If time permits, kids can close their eyes while you hide the squares again. Then play the game again.

Discussion Questions

1. **What are some great things God has done that we read about in the Bible?** (helped the Israelites escape from Pharaoh's army, helped the Israelites get to the Promised Land, healed people, sent Jesus to die for our sins)

2. **What are some great things God has done for you and your family?** You may want to give your own answer as well as inviting volunteers to respond.

3. **Will you praise God for the ways He helps you? How?**

Musical Cans

Bible Focus ▶ Acts 16:16–40

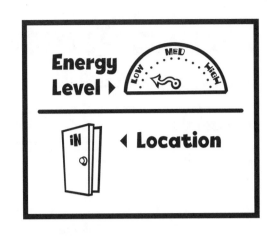

IN ◀ **Location**

Materials
children's music from your collection, music player, empty soda can (1 per student)

Lead the Game
1. **One of the ways to give thanks to God is by singing and making music to God. Paul and Silas were put in jail for teaching about Jesus. While in jail, they prayed and sang hymns. In our game, we're going to play music and answer questions about thanking God.**
2. Play a game with students similar to Musical Chairs. Have kids form a large circle, standing about 1' apart. Give each student a soda can to place at his or her feet. Ask one volunteer to put his or her can to the side of the playing area, away from the circle.
3. Start the music. Students should begin to walk clockwise around the cans. When you stop the music, each student picks up the closest can. The student left without a can answers one of the discussion questions. Continue playing as time allows.

Option
You could substitute index cards in a variety of colors for the soda cans.

Discussion Questions
1. **What are some things you should thank God for?**
2. **Why should we give thanks to God in good times?**
   (We can thank God for letting us have good times.)
3. **Why should we give thanks to God even in hard times?**
   (We can thank God for always being with us. We can trust that God will help us through hard times.)

Pickup Praise

Bible Focus ▶ Acts 2:42–47

◀ **Location**

Materials
3" squares of construction paper (at least 10 squares per student), markers, timer

Lead the Game
1. **As the early church grew, the first Christians spent time praising God. When we worship and praise God, other people may learn about Him and come to praise Him too! Let's play a game to name reasons we have for praising and worshipping God.**
2. Give each student ten squares of paper and a marker. Students should number their paper squares one to ten. Then they should randomly place the squares on the floor, numbered side down, spreading out the squares as much as possible throughout the playing area.

3. Divide the group into two teams. Teams are to line up shoulder-to-shoulder on opposite sides of the playing area. Assign numbers to students as in the game Steal the Bacon (see sketch).
4. Call out two numbers. The kids with those numbers from each team have five seconds to collect as many construction-paper squares as possible. Call, "Stop," when time is up. Students are to return to their teams with the squares they collected and add together the numbers written on the squares. Ask the team with the highest number to tell a reason to praise and worship God.
5. To play another round, students should return the squares to the playing area, numbered side down. Play as many rounds as time allows.

Discussion Questions
1. **When do you worship God? What have you done to worship God today?**
2. **How do you like to praise God?**
3. **When have you seen someone else worship and praise God? What were they doing?**

Praise Phrases

Bible Focus ▶ Luke 17:11–19

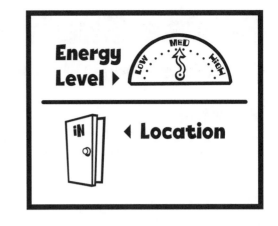

Materials

index cards, marker, a cardboard box for every group of 4 to 6 students, paper, pencils

Preparation

On the index cards, print individual words that can be used in giving praise to God: *I*, *we*, *give*, *thanks*, *God*, *love*, *gifts*, *help*, *sing*, *joy*, *your*, *Son*, *food*, and so forth. Prepare at least three cards for each student, repeating words as needed. Place cardboard boxes around the playing area.

Lead the Game

1. **When Jesus healed ten men who had leprosy and sent them away, only one came back and praised God for His gift of healing. God's gifts should bring us joy and cause our thankfulness to overflow! Let's play a game to give God thanks and praise for all His good gifts!**

2. Give each student at least three cards. Help kids get into groups of four to six students.
3. Each group is to stand around a cardboard box, 3' to 5' from their box. Students should take turns tossing cards, like Frisbees, into the box, tossing each card only once.
4. When the kids have finished tossing the cards, students in each group should collect the cards that landed in their box and use the words to form sentences praising God. Let kids in each group tell their favorite praise sentences to the rest of the students. Then ask the discussion questions.

Discussion Questions

1. **What are some good gifts God gives us?** (family, friends, food, animals, the sun, Jesus, salvation)
2. **What can you do to praise and thank God for these gifts?** (I can praise and thank Him when I talk to Him in prayer. I can tell other people how great He is. I can sing songs of thankfulness to Him.)
3. **When are some times you can praise and thank God?** (before going to bed, on my way to school, at church, before eating.)

Praise Shuffle

Bible Focus ▶ Mark 11:1–11; Philippians 2:10–11

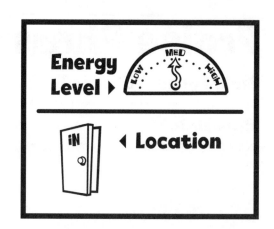

◀ Location

Materials

Bibles, 12" x 18" sheets of green construction paper, scissors, marker, jar lids, whiteboard, dry-erase marker

Preparation

Cut large palm branches from the green construction paper. Divide them into sections to make game boards (see sketch). Make one for every four students. Label the palm branches as shown.

Lead the Game

1. **When Jesus entered Jerusalem on a donkey, people lined the road and praised Him. Let's play a game about praising Jesus!**

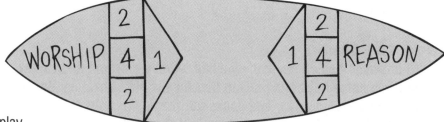

2. Divide the class into two groups to play a game like shuffleboard. Place a game board on the table or floor. Invite a volunteer from one group to place a jar lid upside down at one end of the game board and flick it to the other end. If the lid lands in the Reason space, ask: **Why do you think people praise Jesus?** (He is the Savior. He loves us. He cares for us. He answers our prayers.) List students' ideas on the board. If the lid lands in the Worship space, ask: **What are some ways people worship Jesus?** (sing praise songs to Him, listen as God's Word is taught, give offerings to the church and others who need it, spend time helping others, read and do what the Bible says) Add kids' ideas on the board. If the lid lands on a number space, the team earns that number of points. Keep track of points on the board. Repeat the action with a volunteer from the other team flicking the lid from the opposite end of the game board.

3. Continue the game for several rounds. **Another way to praise Jesus is by reading Bible praises aloud to Him.** Ask the team that scored the highest number of points to read Philippians 2:10–11 aloud together. **How do these verses describe worshiping Jesus?**

Discussion Questions

1. **Some people bow before kings and other important people to show respect. Why does Philippians 2:10–11 tell us to worship Jesus in this way?** (He is Lord of Lords. He is the one true king. Bowing before Him shows how much we respect Him.)
2. **What does it mean for our tongues to acknowledge that Jesus is Lord?** (We tell others that Jesus is important in our lives. We talk about Jesus with respect.)
3. **How can you "acknowledge that Jesus Christ is Lord?"**

Praise Squares

Bible Focus ▸ Daniel 2

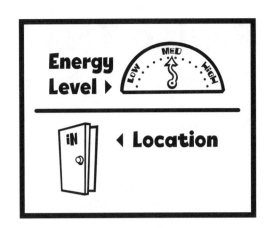

Energy Level ▸   ◂ Location

Materials
index cards, marker, masking tape, rubber ball (or beach ball), whistle

Preparation
Print one letter of the alphabet on each index card, excluding the letters Q, X, and Z. Make one large masking-tape square on the floor of the playing area, then divide the square into four sections. Mix up the alphabet cards, and place a stack of five or six cards near each section.

Lead the Game

1. **Daniel praised God for giving him the ability to interpret dreams for the king. Daniel prayed and praised God. When we pray to God, we can worship Him for how wise and powerful He is and what He has done. In our game today, let's think about some of the reasons that we can worship God.**
2. Lead kids in a game like Foursquare. Students should stand around the outside edges of the square.
3. Give the ball to a student, who then bounces the ball to another student. That student catches the ball and bounces it to another student. Kids continue bouncing the ball. After a short time, blow the whistle. The student holding the ball takes an index card from the nearest stack of cards. That student is to tell something God has done or made that begins with the letter on the card. Then the student returns the card to the bottom of the stack.
4. Continue playing the game as time permits.

Discussion Questions
1. **In our world today, who are some people who often receive praise?** (athletes, movie stars, singers)
2. **Why is it important to praise God?** (God is greater than anyone else. God made everything. We want to tell God we love Him and how glad we are about all the things He has done for us.)
3. **What do you want to praise God for today?** You might want to give your own answer to this question before inviting volunteers to answer.

Praise Toss

Bible Focus ▸ 2 Chronicles 5–7

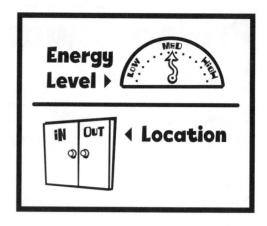

Energy Level ▸

iN OUT ◂ Location

Materials

beach ball (or other soft ball)

Lead the Game

1. **After Solomon had built God's temple, he prayed and he praised God for giving the people a place to worship. God has done so many great things for which we can worship Him! Let's play a game to joyfully name some of the great things God has done.**
2. Have kids stand in a large circle. Assign each student a number.
3. Stand in the center of the circle with the ball. As you toss the ball into the air, call out one of the numbers you assigned. The student whose number you called is to catch the ball and name a reason to thank God or say one thing that God has done or made.
4. After that, the student tosses the ball into the air and calls out another number. The student whose number is called is to catch the ball and name a reason to thank God or say one thing that God has done or made. The game continues as time allows.

Options

1. During the game, list the reasons or things that students name. When you're done playing the game, gather together for a prayer time. Tell students to refer to the list and thank God and celebrate the great things He has done.
2. If you have more than 20 students, form two circles to play the game.
3. To add variety, call out, "Circle switch" several times during the game. At that signal, all students must move to new positions in the circle, but keep their same numbers.

Discussion Questions

1. **What are your favorite parts of God's creation?**
2. **What are some things you have learned about God from the Bible? What are some of the great things God has done for you or people you know?**
3. **What are some ways you can praise God and thank Him for all these wonderful things?** (sing to Him, pray to Him)

Big Book of Bible Games
for Elementary Kids
© David C Cook. Permission granted to photocopy for ministry purposes only.

Search-abilities

Bible Focus ▶ 1 Thessalonians 5:18

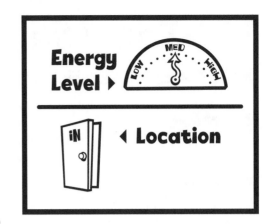

Energy Level ▶

iN ◀ Location

Materials
Bibles, construction paper in a variety of colors, marker, scissors

Preparation
Print "Praise God" on construction paper. Make one paper for each team of no more than eight students. Cut each paper into eight or more puzzle pieces. Hide the pieces around the room.

Lead the Game
1. **God has given each of us abilities—things we're good at or we like to do. Let's play a game using our different skills and abilities to find one great reason to use our abilities.**
2. Divide the class into teams of no more than eight students. Have teams line up on one side of the classroom. Assign each team a color.
3. Call out an ability: read, play piano, kick a soccer ball, sing, and so forth. The first student in each line pantomimes that ability while he or she looks for a puzzle piece of the assigned color. When a student finds a puzzle piece, he or she returns to his or her team, still pantomiming the ability. Then the second student in line takes a turn.
4. After several students have taken their turns, call out a different ability. Students who are looking for puzzle pieces begin pantomiming the new ability. Continue changing abilities frequently until the groups find all their puzzle pieces. Once groups have collected all their puzzle pieces, they should put their puzzles together to discover the phrase Praise God.

Option
Ask older students to help lead the activity by calling out different abilities.

Discussion Questions
1. **What are some ways of praising God? How might a kid your age praise God in one of those ways?** (play or sing a song of praise, read aloud a Bible verse praising God, praise God while praying)
2. **What are some ways you've seen people in your family use their abilities to praise God?**
3. Have a volunteer read 1 Thessalonians 5:18 aloud. **How can you "give thanks in all circumstances"?** (be thankful even when things don't go the way I think they should go, give thanks in the good times and in the bad times)

Tic-Tac-Toe Praise

Bible Focus ▶ 1 Chronicles 15–16

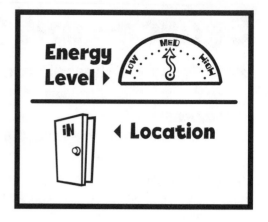

Energy Level ▶

◀ Location iN

Materials

construction paper, marker, masking tape

Preparation

Print the following gifts from God on separate sheets of construction paper: forgiveness, family, prayer, love, courage, talents, salvation, Jesus, power. Use masking tape to make a large tic-tac-toe grid in the playing area. Place one paper, words facedown, in each section of the grid.

Lead the Game

1. **After David had the ark of God brought to Jerusalem, he wrote a psalm that praised God for all His gifts to His people. A great way to celebrate and praise God together as His family is to remember all the good gifts He has given us. Let's play tic-tac-toe to help us remember God's gifts!**

2. Divide the class into two equal teams. Assign one team X and one team O. Volunteers from each team take turns choosing sections of the tic-tac-toe grid to stand in with their arms in X or O shapes (see sketch). Teams are to continue taking turns until one team has three students standing in a row or until all sections of the grid are occupied.

3. Invite a volunteer from the winning team (or the team who had the last turn) to choose one of the papers on which a team member is standing. That team member turns the paper over and reads the word aloud. Then ask another member of that team to tell a way that God has given that gift or a way that we can praise God for that gift.

4. Repeat the game as time permits, with volunteers turning over different cards at the end of each round.

Discussion Questions

1. **What has God given to show His love for you? How has God given you courage? When has God forgiven you?**

2. **Why is it important to praise and thank God for the gifts He has given us?** (to remember that God is good, to recognize that God is the only one who can give such good gifts)

3. **What are some ways we can praise God together?** (sing praise songs, read Bible verses that praise God, say prayers of praise to God)

Big Book of Bible Games
for Elementary Kids
© David C Cook. Permission granted to photocopy for ministry purposes only.

Life Application Games

Prayer

Practice, Practice!

Bible Focus ▶ Daniel 6

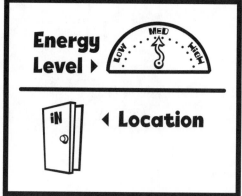

Energy Level ▶

◀ Location

Materials
masking tape, tape measure, materials for one or more of the activities below

Preparation
Set up one or more of the activities below.

Lead the Game
1. **Daniel prayed to God three times a day. Talking to God is so important! The more we pray, the more we get to know God and the ways that we can love and obey Him. Let's practice doing some things several times to see if we get better at them!**
2. Explain the activities. Kids can move around to the different activities as time allows. Make sure that students try the chosen activity more than once so that they get to practice it.

Beanbag Toss
Set a large plastic bowl or tub about 5' from a masking-tape line. Students are to stand behind the line, with their faces turned away from the tub. Kids are to try to get a beanbag into the tub—without looking!

Ball Bounce
Place a clean and empty trash can (or laundry basket) about 8' away from a masking-tape line. Students are to stand behind the line and throw the ball to bounce it into the trash can. The ball must bounce at least once before it enters the trash can.

Marshmallow Move
Set an open bag of marshmallows and a pair of chopsticks 4' from a plastic bowl. Kids are to use chopsticks to pick up a marshmallow and carry it to the plastic bowl, without touching the marshmallow with their hands.

Discussion Questions
1. **Which activity was the hardest? The easiest?**
2. **How did the activities become easier the more you practiced them?**
3. **What could help you remember to pray every day?** (get a reminder from my parents, put an alarm on my phone, do it at the same time every day)

Prayer Hop

Bible Focus ▶ Matthew 6:9–13

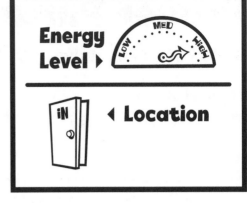

Materials
Bibles, index cards, marker, masking tape, 4 chairs

Preparation
Divide the Lord's Prayer (Matt. 6:9–13) into ten phrases. Print each phrase on a separate index card. Make a duplicate set of cards. Make a masking-tape line on one side of the room. Place chairs in two rows of two in the center of the playing area, one row for each team. Place five cards on each chair, using one set for each team.

Lead the Game
1. **Jesus taught us how important it is to pray to God. Let's play a game to help us remember what Jesus said in the prayer that He prayed as an example for us.**
2. Divide the class into two teams of five students each. Teams are to line up behind the masking-tape line. At your signal, the first student in each line hops to each chair in his or her line, picking up the top card on each stack. The student then returns to tag the next student in line. Continue until all cards have been collected.
3. When a team has collected all its cards, team members should put the cards in order, referring to Matthew 6:9–13 in their Bibles. The first team to finish can read the prayer aloud. Repeat the relay as time permits.

Option
Bring a snack for the students. Before playing the game, draw a small star on one of the cards. At the end of the game, the student who gets the card with the star serves a snack to all students.

Discussion Questions
1. **What are some things Jesus prayed about? What did Jesus ask His Father in heaven to do?**
2. **What are some things you can talk to God about?** (problems at school, family members I'm thankful for, things I need help with)
3. **What are some things you can thank and praise God for? What are some things you need God to help you with?**

Prayer Phrases

Bible Focus ▸ Matthew 6:9–13

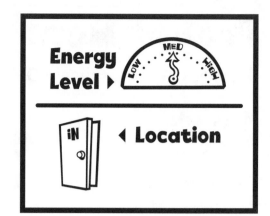

Energy Level ▸

iN ◂ Location

Materials
Bibles, 2 chairs, index cards, marker

Preparation
Write true and false phrases of the Lord's prayer, one phrase per card. (Examples: Our Father in heaven. Our Father in church. Give us today our daily bread. Give us today our daily pizza.) Mix up the cards.

Lead the Game
1. **Jesus taught us how to pray with a prayer we call the Lord's Prayer. Today we're going to play a game to help us learn this prayer.**
2. Divide the class into two equal teams. Have each team sit in a row on the ground so that the two teams are facing each other with about 4' between them. Place chairs as shown in the sketch. Designate one chair to be the "yes" chair, and the other chair to be the "no" chair.
3. Assign a number to each student, assigning the same series of numbers to each team.
4. Explain to students that you'll be reading phrases. Some of the phrases come from the Lord's Prayer and some don't. After you read a phrase, you'll call out a number. The students with those numbers are to decide either "yes," the phrase is part of the Lord's Prayer, or "no," the phrase is not part of the Lord's Prayer. The kids with the numbers are to get up and try to be the first to sit in the chair that represents the correct answer. The kid who sits in the correct chair first scores a point for his or her team.

Option
If you have mostly younger students, give each student his or her own number. When you ask a question, call out one of the numbers. The student with that number sits in the appropriate chair to answer the question.

Discussion Questions
1. Ask volunteers to read Matthew 6:9–13 aloud. **How does saying this prayer help you know about God's love for you?** (God takes care of my important needs. God forgives me when we sin.)
2. **How does knowing this prayer help you at home? At school? With friends?** (It helps me forgive others. It helps me avoid a fight at school.)

Prayer Sentences

Bible Focus ▶ Nehemiah 2:1–5

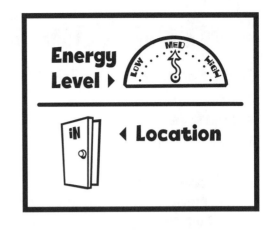

Materials
Bibles, paper, markers, self-stick notes (Optional: masking tape)

Preparation
Print the sentence "God answers my prayer" on a sheet of paper.

Lead the Game
1. **Nehemiah prayed to God, asking for help in rebuilding the torn-down walls of Jerusalem. When we pray, we can tell God things that have happened to us and ask for His help. Let's play a game to help us remember to pray and to know that God answers our prayers.**
2. Give each student a self-stick note. Assign each student a word from the sentence "God answers my prayer," repeating words as needed. Each student is to write his or her assigned word on the self-stick note and then put the note on his or her back. (Optional: Use masking tape to securely attach notes.)
3. Students should begin moving around the playing area. At your signal, students should form groups and line up in order to spell out the sentence. The students who form the sentence first are the winners.
4. Repeat the game as time permits.

Options
1. Students attach self-stick notes to legs, arms, or feet.
2. If space is limited, students can move around the playing area by hopping, jumping, or taking tiny steps.

Discussion Questions
1. Ask a volunteer to read Nehemiah 2:1–5 aloud. **What did Nehemiah pray for?** (that the king would allow him to rebuild Jersualem)
2. **What are some things you should pray about?**
3. **When are some times you can pray?**

Watch Your Back!

Bible Focus ▸ Acts 12:1–17; Colossians 4:2

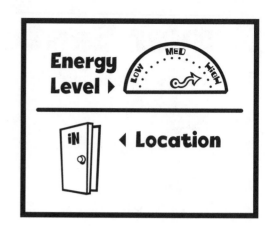
Energy Level ▸ LOW MED HIGH

Location ◂ iN

Materials
large self-stick notes

Lead the Game

1. **God provided an angel to free Peter from prison. God always answers our prayers, though sometimes He does it in ways we don't expect. That's why Colossians 4:2 tells us we need to be watching for the ways He answers. Let's play a game in which we need to be watchful too!**

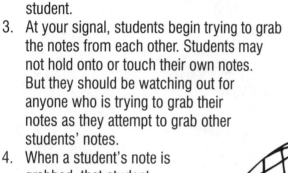

2. Place a self-stick note on the back of each student.

3. At your signal, students begin trying to grab the notes from each other. Students may not hold onto or touch their own notes. But they should be watching out for anyone who is trying to grab their notes as they attempt to grab other students' notes.

4. When a student's note is grabbed, that student must surrender any other notes he or she has collected and then move to the side of the playing area. Grabbing of the notes continues until only one student has his or her original note (and everyone else's notes) or time is called. Redistribute the self-stick notes and play again as time allows.

Option
Instead of using self-stick notes, play the game with long, narrow fabric strips that students tuck into their clothing.

Discussion Questions

1. **What did you watch for while you played this game? What happened if you didn't watch?**

2. **Because we know God always answers prayer, what should we do after we pray about something?** (be watching for how God answers my prayer, not worry about what we've prayed about, trust God to take care of me)

3. **What kinds of things should we talk to God about when we pray?** (things we are thankful for, reasons we love Him, problems we're having, other people who need God's help)

Life Application Games

Serving Others

Amazing Feet

Bible Focus ▶ John 13:1–17

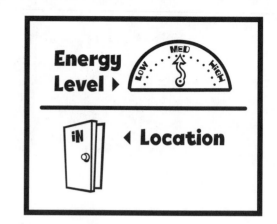

Energy Level ▶

◀ Location

Materials
2 long lengths of roll paper, crayons

Preparation
In an open area of the room, place the lengths of roll paper and crayons on the floor.

Lead the Game
1. **Jesus showed His love to His disciples and served them by washing their feet during the last meal He ate with them. Let's play a game where we serve each other too!**
2. Ask kids to take off their shoes and place them in a large pile on one side of the playing area. Group students into two equal teams. Assign each team a paper that's on the floor.
3. Students on each team should line up in pairs. At your signal, the first pair in each line runs to their team's paper. Students should trace each others' feet on the paper and return to their team. Continue until all students have had their feet traced.
4. When tracing is completed, pairs take turns running to the shoe pile. Students must find their partner's shoes (with help from the partner as needed) and put the shoes on their partner's feet. The game continues until all students have had their feet traced and are wearing their shoes.

Options
1. If you have more than 14 to 16 students, form more than two teams and limit each team to 8 students.
2. If a team has an uneven number of students, you can join the fun!

Discussion Questions
1. **What are some ways Jesus loved and served people when He was here on earth?** (He healed people. He fed people. He taught people about God and the best way to live. He washed the disciples' feet.)
2. **How does God show love for us?** (He sent Jesus to die on the cross for our sins. He created lots of good things for us to enjoy. He gives us families and friends. He gave us the Bible.)
3. **What are some ways we can show love?** (be patient with brothers and sisters, help others at school and in the neighborhood, play games fairly)

Fishy Service

Bible Focus ▶ John 6:1–15; Romans 12:13

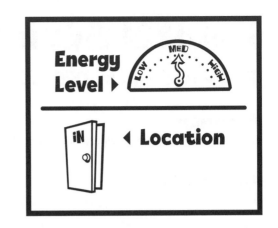

Energy Level ▶

Location ▶ iN

Materials

Bibles, fish-shaped crackers, large bowl, small paper cups

Preparation

Fill the bowl with crackers. Place the bowl on one side of the playing area. (Check for allergies, and prepare an alternate snack as needed.)

Lead the Game

1. **A boy shared his lunch with Jesus. Then Jesus took that lunch and multiplied it to feed thousands of hungry people. Sharing what you have can show your love for God and bring kindness to many people. Let's share some fish crackers in our game today!**
2. Group students into teams of six players. Each team should line up in a single-file line across the playing area from the cracker bowl. Give the first student in each line a small paper cup.
3. At your signal, the first student in each line is to walk quickly to the bowl, scoop out approximately the same number of crackers as there are students on his or her team, and return to his or her team. The student is to let each team member take a cracker from the cup. If the student did not get enough crackers, the student must return to the bowl to get more crackers.
4. The next student in line repeats the action. Play continues until all students on each team have had a turn and have served each team member a cracker.
5. Ask a discussion question to the first team to finish. Continue the discussion with the remaining questions.

Discussion Questions

1. **How do you usually feel when someone shares something with you?** (thankful, special, loved)
2. **Sharing what you have is one way to show kindness. What are some of the things you can share with others at home? At school? With whom can you share these things?**
3. **With whom does Romans 12:13 tell us to share?** Have a student read the verse aloud. (We are to share with God's people who are in need.) Brainstorm with students ways they could share with God's people who are in need.

Helpful Actions

Bible Focus ▶ Acts 11:19–30

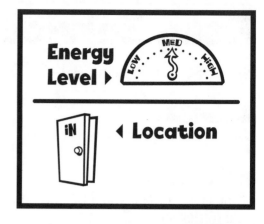

Energy Level ▶

◀ Location

Materials
slips of paper, marker, paper bags, paper plates

Preparation
Print the following words on slips of paper, one word on each paper: *head*, *shoulder*, *hand*, *elbow*, *knee*. Prepare two sets of papers, and put each set into a separate paper bag.

Lead the Game
1. **The people of the early church were persecuted, which means they were treated very badly, for believing in Jesus. But they did what they could to help one another. We can do the same by using what God gives us to help others. Let's help each other play a game using the bodies God has given us!**
2. Group students into teams of no more than eight players. Students within teams should form pairs. (If there is not an even number of students on each team, students can repeat the relay as necessary.) Tell teams to line up in pairs on one side of the room.
3. Give one bag of papers and one paper plate to each team. Have a volunteer from each team choose two slips of paper from his or her team's bag. Tell kids to read the papers aloud. The first pair of students on each team places the paper plate between the two body parts listed on the chosen slips of paper (see sketch).

4. At your signal, the first pair of students on each team walks to the other side of the room and back, keeping the paper plate in position. As pairs return to their teams, the next pair positions the plates in the same way and walks across the room. The relay continues until all pairs have had a turn with the plates in that position. Ask a discussion question to the team that finishes first.
5. Begin a new round of the game with new pairs choosing slips of paper for their teams.

Discussion Questions
1. **What parts of your body can you use to help other people?** (arms, legs, mouth, mind)
2. **What are some ways to help other people using (your arms)?** (carry groceries, fold laundry, hold a crying baby, help with yard work) Repeat the question using other body parts.
3. **What are some ways you can use the money and possessions God has given you and your family to help other people?** (give money to help our church do good things for others, give some of our food and clothing to people who don't have much)

Secret Pass-Off

Bible Focus ▸ Acts 3:1–16

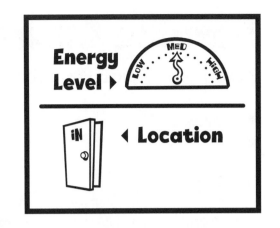

Energy Level ▸

◂ Location

Materials
marbles (or other small objects)

Lead the Game
1. **In the name of Jesus, Peter helped a man who couldn't walk by healing him. Jesus will also help us share what we have to help other people. Let's play a game in which we are secretly trying to give away something!**
2. Choose at least one volunteer to become a "watcher." One watcher for every six or seven kids will be needed. Watchers are to close their eyes while you quietly give marbles or other small objects to no more than half of the remaining students.
3. All students should put their hands behind their backs and begin walking around the room. Kids will pass objects to each other while keeping their hands behind their backs. Watchers, who have their eyes open, will try to find out which students are holding the objects. To make the game harder, all students should pretend to pass objects.
4. Call time after a minute or so. Watchers should name the students they think are holding objects. If their guesses are correct, the kids holding the objects must give them to the watchers. If their guesses are incorrect, begin a new round of play. After the second round, choose new watchers, whether or not all objects have been collected. Play as many rounds as time allows.

Discussion Questions
1. **Was it easier to be a watcher or a secret giver in this game?**
2. **Why does Jesus tell us it's important to give to others?** (Giving or helping others shows we love them. It shows our love for God.)
3. **Besides money, what else can we give to others?** (time, friendship, encouragement)

Serving Charades

Bible Focus ▶ Matthew 25:14–30; Luke 19:12–27

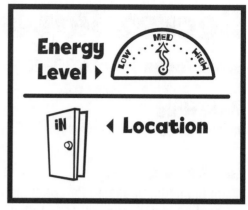

Energy Level ▶

◀ Location

Materials
large sheet of paper, marker

Lead the Game
1. **Jesus told a story about people who wisely used the bags of gold given to them and some people who did not wisely use the bags of gold given to them. In some Bible translations, it talks about "talents" instead of bags of gold. The skills you have, or the things you are good at doing, are sometimes called talents. What are some of the talents you and other kids your age have?** (play a musical instrument, sing, be a good speller, enjoy reading, play soccer) List students' ideas on the large sheet of paper.
2. When you have listed eight to ten talents, play a game similar to Charades. **We can use the talents God gives us to serve others. Let's play a game to act out some of those talents God gives us.** Ask a volunteer to stand in front of the group. Whisper to the volunteer one of the talents from the list. The volunteer should pantomime the talent.
3. The rest of the students are to guess what the volunteer is pantomiming. When students guess correctly, ask: **How can you serve others using this talent?** Extend the discussion using the questions below. Repeat with the other talents on the list, as time allows, or until all students have had a turn to pantomime a talent.

Option
Play Charades as two teams. Whisper to a volunteer from each team one of the talents. At your signal, volunteers should pantomime the talent. The first team to correctly guess the talent wins. Repeat with different volunteers and talents.

Discussion Questions
1. **Why is it true that almost all talents can be used to serve others?** (almost anything we do can be done in a way that shows care for others and love for God)
2. **Why is it important to use the talents God has given you?** (If we don't practice the skills and talents that God gave us, we may lose them.)
3. **What are some ways to use your talents to serve others at church? At school? In the neighborhood?**

Snack Service

Bible Focus ▶ John 13:1–17; Galatians 5:13

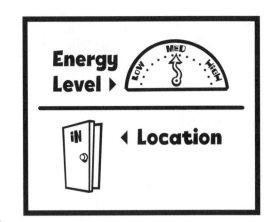

Materials
Bibles, individually wrapped snacks (at least 1 per student), paper plates

Preparation
For each group of five to seven students, place five to seven snacks on a paper plate.

Lead the Game
1. **Jesus showed love to His disciples by washing their feet. Normally, a house servant would have done that. Because we love God, it's important we're ready to serve others. Let's play a game to practice serving others!**
2. Group students into teams of five to seven students each. Teams should line up on one side of the room. Set an empty paper plate next to the first player on each team. Place a plate of snacks across the playing area from each team.

3. At your signal, the first player on each team walks quickly to the other side of the room, retrieves a snack from the team's plate, and brings it back, placing it on the team's empty plate. The next student in line repeats the action, leaving as the first student places the snack on the plate. Play continues until all members of the team have collected a snack.
4. Each student takes a snack from the team's plate and gives it to someone else on the team. After kids have swallowed the snacks, tell them to whistle. The first team that has all its players whistling wins.

Discussion Questions
1. **How did you serve each other in the game?** (gave each other snacks)
2. **How can we serve others at school? At home? On the playground?**
3. **Have a volunteer read Galatians 5:13 aloud. What do you think it means to serve someone in love?** (be kind and humble, don't have a bossy or proud attitude, pay attention to the needs of others)

Toe Service

Bible Focus ▸ John 15:13

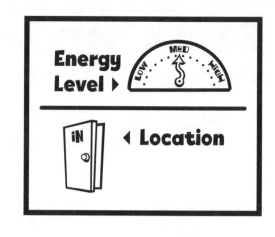

Energy Level ▸

◂ Location

Materials
index cards, marker

Preparation
Print the words of John 15:13 on index cards, one word per card. Make one set of verse cards for every eight to ten students.

Lead the Game
1. **One of the ways Jesus showed His love was to wash His disciples' feet. Washing feet was something that a house servant would normally do. Let's play a game that uses our feet!**
2. Group kids in teams of eight to ten players. Each team is to line up single-file on one side of the playing area. Students should remove their shoes and socks. Place a set of mixed-up verse cards across the playing area from each team.
3. At your signal, the first student from each team skips across the playing area to the cards, picks up one of the cards, and places it between his or her first two toes. The student walks back to his or her team with the card held between toes. If the card falls before he or she returns to the team, the student must stop to put the card back between the toes. The next students in line repeat the action until all the cards have been collected. Students on each team are to work together to put the cards in verse order. Let the first team finished read the verse aloud.

Option
If your class has fewer than 16 students, all students can participate as one team and race against the clock.

Discussion Questions
1. **Jesus showed us His love for us when He died on the cross for our sins. How can we show love to our friends?** (help them even when we don't feel like it, be friendly even if they aren't being very friendly to us, think of a caring thing we can do and do it)
2. **What can we do to thank Jesus for laying down His life for us?** (We can thank Him in our prayers. We can believe in Him and accept His offer of salvation.)

Big Book of Bible Games for Elementary Kids

Life Application Games

Showing Love to God

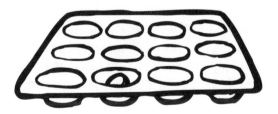

Ability Blast

Bible Focus ▶ Matthew 25:14–30

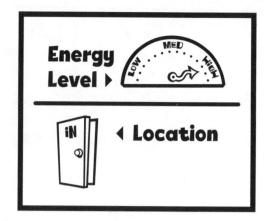

Energy Level ▶

iN ◀ Location

Materials
Bibles, index cards, marker, children's music from your collection, music player, tape

Preparation
Print each of the following abilities on separate index cards: play baseball, play piano, math skills, spell, compete in gymnastics, write, read, play soccer, draw, sing, act, run.

Lead the Game
1. **Jesus told a story about some people who used what they were given wisely and a person who didn't. We can show our love to God by wisely using the abilities He has given us. Let's play a game to think of some of those abilities and how we can be faithful in using them!**
2. Play music as students walk around the room. When you stop the music, each student should quickly move to a corner of the room, making sure there is approximately the same number of students in each corner.
3. Tape an index card in each corner. The students in each corner should read the card and plan a way to pantomime the ability. Groups take turns pantomiming abilities for the other groups to guess. Ask a discussion question after abilities have been guessed.
4. At the end of each round of play, collect the cards and repeat the game as time allows, distributing a new set of ability cards each round.

Discussion Questions
1. **What does it mean to be faithful?** (to keep doing something you said you would do, to keep your promises)
2. **How does Colossians 3:23 describe being faithful?** Have a volunteer read the verse aloud. (doing something with your whole heart; doing something that pleases God, not just to please the people around you)
3. **What are some ways to be faithful in using the abilities God has given to you?** (practice using those abilities, keep using them to help others, have a good attitude while using your abilities, use your abilities to please God)

Add-a-Fruit Relay

Bible Focus ▸ Galatians 5:22–23

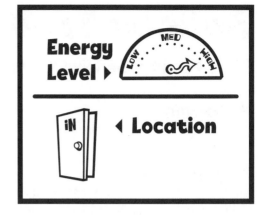

Energy Level ▸ LOW MED HIGH

iN ◂ **Location**

Materials
Bibles, marker, colored paper, roll paper, masking tape, scissors, pencils

Preparation
Draw a fruit shape (apple, banana, orange, pear, lemon) on colored paper. The shape should be large enough for students to write on. On a length of roll paper, draw the outline of a large, leafy tree. Attach the paper to the wall or place it on the floor on one side of the playing area.

Lead the Game
1. **Growing the fruit of the Spirit in our lives begins with love for God. Let's play a game to learn more about the fruit of the Spirit!**
2. Divide the group into equal teams. Ask each student to cut out a fruit shape. Then ask a volunteer to Galatians 5:22–23 aloud. Assign each student the name of one of the fruit of the Spirit to write on his or her shape. Students should then attach masking-tape loops to the backs of their shapes.
3. Have teams line up in single-file lines across the room from the tree. At your signal, students on each team take turns running to the tree and attaching a shape to it. Then they return to the team and tag the next student in line. Play continues until each student has attached a fruit shape. Tell teams to sit down as they finish.
4. Ask a discussion question to the first team that finishes or let them say Galatians 5:22–23 together. Repeat the relay as time permits.

Option
To simplify preparation, have each student draw a fruit on a self-stick note and write the name of a fruit of the Spirit on the note. Students use the self-stick notes instead of the fruit shapes in the relay.

Discussion Questions
1. **Which fruit of the Spirit, in Galatians 5:22–23, is most needed by kids your age?**
2. **How has someone that you know shown a fruit of the Spirit?**
3. **When might a kid your age show love? Patience? Joy?** Repeat with other fruit of the Spirit as time allows.

Balloon Trolley

Bible Focus ▸ Genesis 4:1–4; 1 Chronicles 16:29

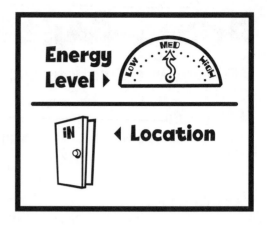

Energy Level ▸

iN ◂ Location

Materials

balloons, garbage bag, chairs

Preparation

Inflate one balloon for every pair of students, plus several extras. You can transport the inflated balloons to class in a garbage bag. Place several chairs about 3' from the edge of one side of the playing area. Make sure that chairs are at least 4' from each other and that there are approximately two chairs for every eight students.

Lead the Game

1. **Abel offered a gift to God that was the best he could give. We can show thankfulness to God by offering Him our love, time, abilities, and money. Let's play a game to think of ways to offer God those things!**
2. Have students form pairs and give each pair a balloon. Students in pairs are to decide the best way to hold the balloon between themselves without touching it with their hands (between hips, between upper arms, between back and stomach). Let the pairs practice moving around the room in the manner chosen.
3. Invite pairs to stand opposite the chairs. Tell the pairs to position the balloon in the manner chosen. At your signal, all pairs should move toward the chairs, walk around one chair, and return to the starting position without dropping the balloons. The first pair back to the starting side names a way to show thankfulness to God. Repeat play as time allows, with the first pair finished telling a way to give God their time or a way to give God their money. You can also ask teams the discussion questions.

Discussion Questions

1. **How can kids your age give their time as an offering to God?** (play with a brother or sister instead of doing something else, help clean up trash in their neighborhood)
2. **When have you or your family given money or other things you own to show thankfulness to God?** (gave money to a missionary family, gave food to people who didn't have much)
3. **Why is it important to give offerings to God?** (helps us remember God's gifts to us)

Big Book of Bible Games
for Elementary Kids
© David C Cook. Permission granted to photocopy for ministry purposes only.

Bread, Basket, Fish

Bible Focus ▸ Mark 6:30–44; John 6:1–15

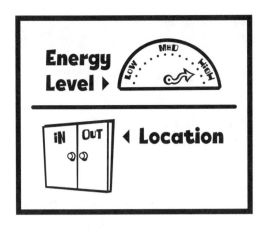

Materials
large sheet of paper, marker

Lead the Game
1. **When we give to God, He can do great things with our gifts to Him. A boy once gave his small lunch to Jesus. Jesus used this small lunch to feed a huge crowd. Let's play a game to remind ourselves of the gifts given by this boy.**
2. Have kids form two teams and stand in the center of a large playing area. Designate a safe zone (wall, door) for each team, one on each end of the playing area.

bread
basket
fish

3. Play a large-group version of Rock, Paper, Scissors using the words *bread*, *basket*, and *fish* and these signs: bread—fist, basket—two hands cupped together, fish—two palms pressed together swimming like a fish (see sketch). Basket defeats bread, because bread is put into the basket. Bread defeats fish, because bread is wrapped around fish for eating. Fish defeats basket, because live fish can flop out of the basket. Write the signs and scoring system on a large sheet of paper to which students can refer.
4. Each team huddles near its safe zone and chooses one sign. Then, after moving to the center of the playing area, all members of each team say "Bread, basket, fish" aloud in unison and show their team's chosen sign. The winning team chases the losing team back toward the losing team's safe zone. Any student who is tagged joins the winning team. If both teams show the same sign, the teams should huddle and play again. Repeat the game as time permits, with team members taking turns choosing their team's sign.

Option
Play the game in pairs. After the first round, each winner plays another winner and each loser plays another loser. The game is over when one student has won five rounds. Play as many games as time and interest permit.

Discussion Questions
1. **What did Jesus do with the boy's bread and fish?**
2. **What can we give to God to show love for Him?** (actions that show obedience to God, time when we pray to Him or read His Word, money to help others)
3. **What might God do with what we offer to Him?** (God might use what we offer to help others learn about Him. God might use what we offer to help someone not feel sad.)

Faithfulness Toss

Bible Focus ▸ Daniel 3

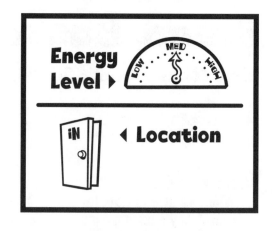

Energy Level ▸

iN ◀ Location

Materials
2 muffin tins, paper, pencil, coins

Lead the Game
1. **Daniel showed his love for God by refusing to pray to anyone other than God. Acting in ways that show belief in God demonstrates our faithfulness and love for God. Let's play a game to name some ways to show belief in God.**
2. Divide the group into two equal teams, and ask each team to line up. Place a muffin tin about 4' from each team. Give one volunteer on each team a sheet of paper and a pencil to record points.
3. Give two coins to the first student in each line. The student tosses the coins, one at a time, at his or her team's muffin tin. If a coin goes into a cup, the team scorekeeper records one point. Continue until each student has had a turn.
4. One or two times during the game call, "Stop." A volunteer from the team with the most points tells one way to show belief in and faithfulness to God. (pray to God, read the Bible, tell the truth, tell others about God, obey God) Repeat the game as time allows.

Options
1. Instead of using muffin tins, use clean yogurt cups or draw circles on a large sheet of paper.
2. Label small, circular stickers from one to five. Attach a sticker to bottom of each muffin tin cup. Students earn the number of points on the sticker.
3. Instead of tossing coins, students place marshmallows or gummy fruits onto plastic spoons and fling them at muffin tins.

Discussion Questions
1. **How does (praying) show you believe in God?** (I am trusting God to hear me and answer my prayers.) Repeat the question with different actions that show belief in God.
2. **When are some times you have seen other people show their belief in God?** You might want to share your own answer before you ask for responses from students.
3. **How can you show faithfulness to God when you are with your friends? When you are with your family?**

Paper-Chain Relay

Bible Focus ▸ Hebrews 11:1—12:2

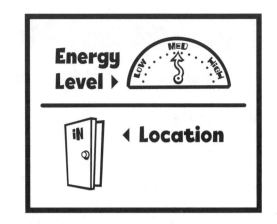

Energy Level ▸

iN ◂ **Location**

Materials
Bibles, paper, scissors, ruler, tape (or staplers), markers

Preparation
Cut paper into strips 2" wide, making at least two for each student. Make piles of 12 to 16 strips on one side of the playing area. Next to each pile, place tape or a stapler.

Lead the Game
1. **When we remember the actions of the people in God's family, we are encouraged to show faith in God. Let's play a game to help us remember that we can all be part of that family and to help us think about ways others help us to love and obey God.**
2. Group students into teams of no more than six to eight players. Teams should line up in single-file lines across the playing area from the piles of paper strips.
3. Give the first student in each line a marker. At your signal, the first student from each team runs to his or her team's pile and writes his or her name on a paper strip. The student tapes or staples it into a loop. The student leaves the loop and returns to his or her team, giving the marker to the next student in line. That student repeats the action, looping his or her strip through the first student's loop to create a paper chain. Teams continue until all students have had a turn.
4. Play another round of the relay, this time asking each student to write on the paper the name of a person who taught him or her about God.
5. Connect the paper chains and display them in the classroom as a visual reminder of people in God's family. Have a volunteer read Hebrews 12:1–2 aloud.

Discussion Questions
1. **What stories about Bible people help you want to love and obey God?**
2. **How can kids your age show faith in God?** (do what God says to do, pray to God and ask for His help in showing love, believe in God no matter what others say)
3. **Who is someone you know who loves and obeys God? What can you learn from that person's example?** (I can learn to tell the truth. I can learn to thank God for His forgiveness.)

Perpetual Motion

Bible Focus ▶ Daniel 1; 6; Mark 12:30

Materials
Bibles, 2 Frisbees

Energy Level ▶

◀ Location

Lead the Game
1. **Loving and obeying God your whole life are the wisest things to do! Daniel loved and obeyed God his whole life, even when it meant disobeying the king. Let's play a game in which we try to keep something going for a long time.**
2. Divide the group into two equal teams. Ask the teams to line up at one end of room. Place Frisbees at the opposite end of the room across from each team.
3. At your signal, the first player in line high-fives the next player in line, who high-fives the next player, and so on down the line. After receiving a high-five, the last player in line runs to his or her team's Frisbee and spins it on its edge. The player then runs to the front of the line and keeps the motion going by high-fiving the next player in line and so on. Players shift down one position in line as each runner returns. The first team to get its players back in their original position wins.
4. Ask the winning team to answer this question: **What is one way a kid your age can love and obey God?** Repeat the game as time permits.

Options
1. Instead of Frisbees, students could spin two sturdy paper plates stapled face-to-face.
2. Limit the number of students on each team to six or seven. Provide additional Frisbees if more teams are needed.

Discussion Questions
1. **Why are loving and obeying God our whole lives the wisest things we can do?** (God tells us the best ways to live. Loving and obeying God is what we were created to do.)
2. **How did Daniel show he loved and obeyed God?** (He had the courage to ask for and eat vegetables rather than what the king commanded him to eat. He prayed to God, even when another king outlawed it.)
3. Have a volunteer read Mark 12:30 aloud. **What can you do to show that you love and obey God?** (praise Him with songs and in prayers, obey God's commands, make God number one)

Sharing Love

Bible Focus ▶ Mark 12:41–44;
Luke 20:45–47; 21:1–4

Energy Level ▶ LOW MED HIGH

◀ **Location** iN

Materials
2 coins for each student, 1 or more of each of the following containers:
paper plates, paper cups, coffee cans, plastic bowls

Preparation
Set out the containers, and make a masking-tape square as shown in
the sketch. (If you have more than 16 kids, make additional squares with additional containers in them.)

Lead the Game
1. **In the Bible we read about a poor woman who showed she loved God by generously giving her last two coins. Let's play a game with coins and think about how we can give generously to God as a way of thanking Him for His love.**
2. Give each student two coins, and have kids stand around the square. Students are to take turns tossing coins, trying to get the coins into the containers. When a student's coin lands in a container, he or she tells a way to give to God or to others (donate food to people in need, treat others kindly, pray for others, and so forth). After each student has had a turn, collect the coins and redistribute them. Kids can trade places around the square and play again. Repeat the game as time permits.

Options
1. Set up the containers on one end of a table. Students line up and toss coins from the opposite end of the table.
2. Place candy or stickers on some of the plates and in the bottom of some of the cans, bowls, and cups. When a student's coin lands in one of these containers, the student gets candy or stickers.

Discussion Questions
1. **What does it mean to give generously?** (to give more than what is required or expected)
2. **What are some ways you can give generously at school? At home?** (help others with what they are learning if they don't understand, give something that's mine to someone else)
3. **How can you give generously to God to show your thankfulness for His love?** (give my time by reading the Bible and praying, give my abilities to help others learn about God)

Tunnel Ball

Bible Focus ▶ Genesis 12:1–9;
15:1–6; 18:1–15; 21:1–7

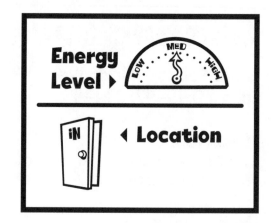

Materials
at least 3 shoeboxes (or other cardboard boxes), scissors, tape measure, marker, masking tape, foam balls (or tennis balls)

Preparation
Cut both ends out of the boxes to form tunnels. Set up tunnels at least
7' from each other, arranging them in a circular course (see sketch). Number each tunnel. Use masking tape to make a start/finish line.

Lead the Game
1. **In the Bible, Abraham had to wait a long time for God to keep His promise to send Abraham a son. We can wait patiently and depend on God to keep His promises, because God always keeps His promises. Let's play a game that might take some patience.**
2. Group students into two teams, and give each team a ball.
3. Students on each team take turns cooperatively rolling the ball around the course from start to finish, with each student allowed one roll at a time. Each student begins his or her turn from where the ball stopped rolling. The ball must pass through each tunnel in order. Have the team that finishes first answer one of the discussion questions.

Options
1. Print each of the following verse references on three index cards, one reference per card: Joshua 1:9; Psalm 29:11; 136:26. Tape one index card on each tunnel. As students roll the balls through the tunnels, a team member finds the verse and reads God's promise aloud.
2. Instead of rolling the balls, each student taps the balls with a toy plastic golf club or a mallet made by taping a dry kitchen sponge to one end of a yardstick.

Discussion Questions
1. **What are some of the promises God has given us in the Bible?** (He will always love us. He will always be with us. He will answer our prayers.)
2. **When might you need to wait patiently for God to keep a promise?** (when praying about a problem, when I need God's help to know what to do)
3. **What might help us to wait patiently for God?** (remember the times He has helped us in the past, thank Him for His love, pray and ask for patience)

Big Book of Bible Games
for Elementary Kids
© David C Cook. Permission granted to photocopy for ministry purposes only.

Life Application Games

Showing Love to Others

"After You"

Bible Focus ▸ Luke 18:9–14; Philippians 2:3

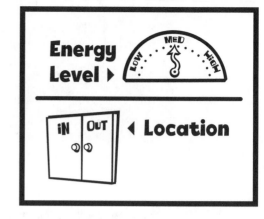

Materials
Bibles, tube socks (1 sock for each pair of students)

Lead the Game
1. **Jesus told a story about a person who humbly asked God for mercy. When we care about others, we remember God's love for them, and our humble and gentle attitudes help us to not look down on them. Let's each practice a humble attitude by putting others first in our game.**
2. Have students form pairs. Pairs should stand on one side of the playing area.
3. Give each pair a tube sock. Partners are to hold the sock between them, each with one hand on the sock. Pairs should practice stepping over the sock, one foot at a time, without letting go of the sock.
4. To begin the game, students are to stand on one side of the playing area. At your signal, one student in the pair says, "After you," and his or her partner takes a step, putting one foot and then the other over the sock. Then the partner who stepped says, "After you," and the other partner takes a turn. Students continue in this manner, moving across the playing area and back.
5. After all pairs have returned to the starting area, ask the pair who finished first to answer one of the discussion questions. Play again as time permits.

Discussion Questions
1. **What are some examples of a humble and gentle attitude?** (letting others go first, not thinking you are better than anyone else, listening carefully when others speak)
2. Have a volunteer read Philippians 2:3 aloud. **What does this verse say about having a humble attitude?** (don't do things because you're trying to get something for yourself or because you think you're better than other people, don't spend too much time thinking about yourself)
3. **When we have humble attitudes, we don't spend time comparing ourselves to others. What should we think about instead?** (ways to love God and others, how we can help others)

Call the Ball

Bible Focus ▶ Acts 4:32—5:11

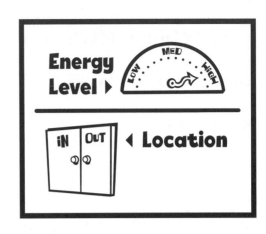

Energy Level ▶

iN | OuT ◀ **Location**

Materials
ball best suited for your playing area (playground ball, tennis ball, Ping-Pong ball, or small rubber ball)

Preparation
Depending on the type of ball you are playing with and the ability of your students, choose three actions from the Action List below.

Lead the Game
1. **A couple in the early church chose to lie about a gift they were giving to God. They said one thing but did another. One way to show our love for God is by making sure our words and actions match. Let's practice matching our words and actions!**
2. Group students into two even teams. (If needed, you can join the fun!) Teams are to line up in single-file lines across the playing area from each other, leaving a wide space between the first player of each team (see sketch).
3. Demonstrate the three actions you chose, identifying each action by name. Give the ball to the first student in one line. The student with the ball calls out one of the actions and moves the ball in that manner to the first student on the other team. The first student on the other team catches the ball and then calls out another action, moving the ball in that manner back to the first team. If the ball does not move in the manner called, the student tries again. The game continues until all kids have had at least one turn to call out an action and move the ball.

Action List
Single bounce, double bounce, or triple bounce: bounce the ball the appropriate number of times
Dribble and toss: dribble the ball halfway across the playing area and then toss the ball
Left-hand bounce or right-hand bounce: bounce the ball with left or right hand
No bounce: toss the ball with no bounce
Grand slam: bounce the ball very high and hard
Baby bounce: bounce the ball low to the ground

Discussion Questions
1. **What does it mean to make your words and your actions match?** (I shouldn't say one thing and then do something else. If I tell someone a good way to act, I should act that way myself.)
2. **What are some ways your words and action can match at home? At school?**
3. **Making our words match our actions is one way to show goodness. How does God help us have the fruit of goodness?** (God gives us the Bible, parents, and teachers to help us understand right ways to act.)

Compassion Corners

Bible Focus ▸ Luke 10:25–37

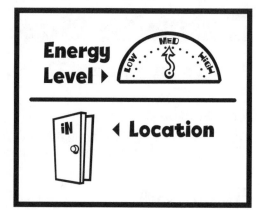

Energy Level ▸

iN ◂ **Location**

Materials
Bibles, 4 sheets of paper, index cards, marker, masking tape, small paper bag

Preparation
Print the words *heart*, *soul*, *mind*, and *strength* on four sheets of paper and four index cards, one word per paper and card. Post each paper in a separate corner of the room. Place index cards in a paper bag.

Lead the Game

1. **Because we have experienced God's great love for us, we can show His love and compassion to others. In our game today, we'll describe ways to show love and compassion every day.**
2. Have a volunteer read Luke 10:27 aloud. **What does this verse describe?** (how we are to love God) Ask volunteers to read aloud the words on the papers in the corners of the room.
3. Have kids stand in a circle. Ask a volunteer to be "It." "It" stands in the middle of the circle. Students should walk around the circle. After a few moments, "It" calls, "Stop!" Students move quickly to the nearest corners. "It" picks an index card from the bag and reads the card aloud before returning the card to bag. A volunteer from the corner named on the index card tells one way to show love or compassion to others, recites Luke 10:27, or answers a discussion question. The student who answered becomes the new "It," and the game continues as time allows.

Discussion Questions
1. **How has God shown His love and compassion for you?** (He sent His Son, Jesus, to die on the cross to forgive my sins. He answers my prayers. He helps me do what's right.) **How can you show your love for God?** (tell Him that I love Him, follow His commands, pray to Him, read the Bible, tell others about Him)
2. **What are some other words or phrases that describe ways of showing love?** (helping, caring, encouraging someone, praying for others, sharing with others)
3. **What are some things you could do to show your love for others at home? At school? In the neighborhood?**

Courage Collection

Bible Focus ▸ 1 Samuel 24; Luke 6:27

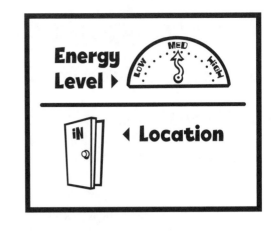

Materials
Bibles, large length of colored roll paper, marker, newspaper, masking tape, 2 bowls, flour, marshmallows, pencils, paper

Preparation
Draw lines to divide the roll paper into at least 12 large sections. In each section, print a number (five or lower) and a word from Luke 6:27, including the reference. Tape the paper to wall. Spread the newspaper on the floor under the paper and out about 4' from the wall. Fill bowls ⅓ full with flour, and place them at the edge of the newspaper.

Lead the Game

1. **In the Old Testament, David demonstrated love for an enemy who was trying to kill him. We think of our enemies as people we don't like, but God can give us the courage to love our enemies! Let's play a game to find out what Jesus said about loving enemies.**
2. Divide the group into two teams. Teams are to line up single file at the edge of the newspaper.
3. Each student is to take a turn dipping a marshmallow into the flour, and then tossing it at the paper. Teams should attempt to hit all sections on the paper to collect each word of the verse and to earn as many points as possible. Have a volunteer from each team write on a sheet of paper which words of the verse have been collected and the number of points earned. Students can refer to their Bibles for verse order. Students are to keep tossing marshmallows until both teams have collected all the words of the verse. Have a volunteer from the first team that finishes read Luke 6:27 aloud or answer one of the discussion questions.

Discussion Questions
1. **What are some ways to show love and do good things for people who you might think of as enemies?** (don't be mean to them, don't say mean things about them to others, smile and be friendly to them)
2. **What can you do when it seems too hard to show God's love to an enemy?** (I can ask God for courage to do what's right. I can ask a parent or teacher for advice on how to show love.)

Crazy Fruit

Bible Focus ▸ Galatians 5:22–23

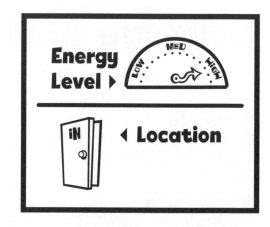

Energy Level ▸

iN ◂ Location

Lead the Game

1. **We show the fruit of the Spirit when we love God and others. Let's play a game to think about ways to show God's love!**
2. Ask kids to sit in a circle. Select a volunteer to be the farmer and stand in the middle of the circle. Assign each student a fruit (banana, strawberry, peach, grape, pineapple, orange, and so forth), making sure to assign each fruit to more than one student.
3. The farmer calls out the name of a fruit. Kids with that fruit jump up to trade places in the circle before the farmer can take one of the places. When the farmer calls out, "Crazy fruit!" all students must change places.
4. The student left without a place becomes the new farmer. Before calling out a fruit name, the farmer tells one way to show love for God or others. Ask discussion questions to guide the discussion as needed. Repeat play as above. The game continues as time allows or until all students have had the opportunity to be the farmer.

Blueberries

Options

Play another round of the game using the names of the fruit of the Spirit from Galatians 5:22–23, instead of using the names of actual fruits. As a review, ask students to name the fruit of the Spirit before assigning them to each student. You may want to list the fruit of the Spirit on the board for students to refer to during the game and the discussion.

Discussion Questions

1. **What can you do to show (patience) to someone you know?** Repeat the question with other fruit of the Spirit. **Practicing the fruit of the Spirit is a way to show love for others.**
2. **What are some ways to show love for God?** (obey Him, sing songs of praise to Him, thank Him when praying, tell others about Him) **How can you show your (faithfulness) to God? How does showing (self-control) demonstrate love for God?**
3. **Who is someone you know who shows love for God and others? How does he or she show that love? What can you do to show love for God or others in that way?**

Frisbee Frenzy

Bible Focus ▸ 2 Kings 4:8–37; 1 John 3:18

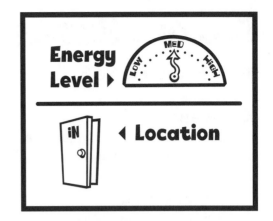

Materials
Bibles, paper plates, markers

Preparation
Divide the playing area in half with a masking-tape line.

Lead the Game
1. **God sent the prophet Elisha to help a poor widow who had a very sick son.**
2. Give each student a paper plate and a marker. **What are things people need?** (food, water, friends, family, help, etc.) Each student should write something people need on his or her plate. Divide the class into two groups. Groups should stand on opposite sides of the room. At your signal, all students are to toss their paper plates Frisbee-style across the room.
3. Each student is to catch or pick up one paper plate. Each student should write on the plate that was caught an example of a way to show God's love to someone with the need that's written on the plate.
4. Tell kids to toss and catch the plates again. Ask several volunteers to read the needs and responses on plates. Using the discussion questions, lead students in discussing words and actions that can be used to show God's love.

Option
After kids have written needs and responses on the paper plates, students should take turns tossing the paper plates into a box or wastebasket. When a plate lands in the box or basket, the student answers a question.

Discussion Questions
1. Have a volunteer read 1 John 3:18 aloud. **Why do you think it's important to show God's love instead of just talking about it?**
2. **What are some words that describe the way people act who show God's love?** (joyful, peaceful, patient, kind, good, faithful, gentle)
3. **What are some ways you can show God's love to someone this week?**

Frozen Poses

Bible Focus ▸ Luke 6:27–28; 7:1–10

Energy Level ▸

iN ◀ **Location**

Materials

Bibles, children's music from your collection, music player (Optional: large sheet of paper, marker)

Lead the Game

1. **What kind of motion would remind you of the word** *friends*? (shaking hands, giving a high-five) **What kind of motion would remind you of the word** *enemies*? (clenched fist, crossed arms) Lead students in choosing a motion for each word.

2. **The Jewish people in Bible times called the Romans their enemies because the Romans ruled over the Jewish people. But one time Jesus healed a Roman ruler's sick servant! Let's talk about some ways we can help people become our friends instead of enemies.** As you play music, students are to move randomly around the room. After playing the music for approximately ten seconds or so, stop the music. Call out either "Friends" or "Enemies." All students must freeze in the appropriate pose. If you called out "Friends," ask a volunteer to tell a way to show God's love and friendship to someone whom others dislike. (Optional: List students' responses on a large sheet of paper.) If you called out "Enemies," ask a volunteer to tell a way to show God's love and friendship to someone who has been mean to him or her. Continue playing the game as time permits. Ask the discussion questions during the music pauses.

3. After playing the game, invite volunteers to tell ways they can show friendship to others during the week. Be sure to also tell kids what you plan to do also.

Discussion Questions

1. Have a volunteer read Luke 6:27–28 aloud. **Why do you think God wants us to love our enemies?** (because God loves everyone)
2. **How can you love your enemies?**
3. **What would happen if kids your age prayed for their enemies?** You might want to give an answer before asking kids to respond.

Good-Sam Relay

Bible Focus ▸ Luke 10:25–37

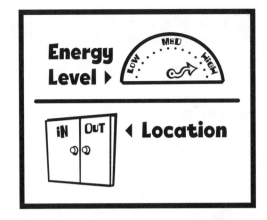

Materials
masking tape, adhesive bandages, basket, 10 coins

Preparation
Using masking tape, make a starting line on the floor. For each team, make an X on the ground with masking tape about 5' from the starting line. About 5' on the ground beyond the X, place a bandage for each player. Near the wall opposite the starting line, place the basket. Set the coins a few feet in front of the basket.

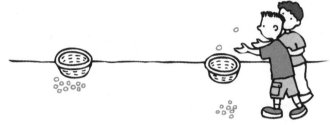

Lead the Game
1. **Let's play a game that will help us remember the story that Jesus told about someone who was traveling to Jericho.**
2. Divide the class into teams, and ask kids to form pairs within the teams. Ask a pair of kids to help you demonstrate how to complete the relay. Partners are to run to the X on the ground. One player lies on the X and represents the hurt man. The other player runs around the player twice. Then partners switch roles. Next, partners run to the bandages, place one bandage on each other, and then run to the basket. Each partner should toss a coin into the basket. Pairs are to run back to their team and then the next pair begins the relay.
3. At your signal, the first pairs run the relay. The first team to complete the course wins. Ask the winning team one or more of the discussion questions, and repeat the game as time allows.

Discussion Questions
1. **Who helped the hurt Jewish man?** (a Samaritan man) **Why was it unusual for someone who was a Samaritan to be kind to a Jewish man?** (Jews and Samaritans did not like each other.)
2. **What did the Samaritan man do that was kind?** (He bandaged the man's wounds, took him to an inn, and paid the innkeeper to take care of the man.)
3. **Why did Jesus tell this story?** (to explain who our neighbors are, to show that we should be kind to anyone in need)

Kindness Circle

Bible Focus ▸ Acts 3:1–10

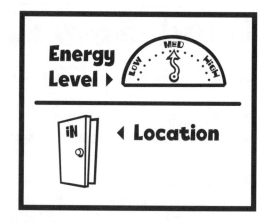

Materials

whiteboard, dry-erase marker, marker, playground ball (or tennis ball)

Lead the Game

1. **Peter showed kind actions by healing a man who couldn't walk. The kind actions we do for others can also demonstrate God's love. In our game we'll show some kind actions!**

2. **What are some kind actions that we can do for others?** (listen to someone who is upset, let someone else be first in line, make a card for someone who is sick) List students' ideas on the board.

3. Choose a volunteer. Other students should stand in a large circle, spreading their legs so that each student's right foot is touching the left foot of the student next to him or her. The volunteer stands in the middle of the circle. Give the ball to the volunteer.

4. The volunteer should roll the ball toward a student in the circle, trying to get the ball between the student's legs. Students in the circle may use their hands to bat away the ball, but they cannot move their feet. If the volunteer gets the ball past a student, that student goes to the middle of the circle and pantomimes a kind action from the list on the board. The rest of the students are to try to guess the kind action being pantomimed. The first student to guess the pantomimed action takes a turn rolling the ball. If the volunteer does not get the ball past the student, the volunteer rolls the ball again. After three unsuccessful tries, the volunteer pantomimes a kind action before a new student is chosen to roll the ball. Continue playing the game as time allows.

Discussion Questions

1. **What are some kind actions you can do at home? At school? In your neighborhood?** (let a friend choose which game to play, empty the dishwasher, invite a new kid to play a game at school)

2. **How can your kind actions help other people learn about God's love?** (They might ask why you are being kind, and you can tell them about God's love.)

3. **What is one kind action you can do this week?**

Kindness Toss

Bible Focus ▸ 2 Kings 4:8–37; Matthew 5:7

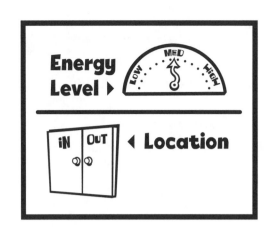

Energy Level ▸

iN OUT ◂ Location

Materials
Bibles, large container, index cards, soft balls (or beanbags), marker

Preparation
Place the container on the floor on one side of the playing area.

Lead the Game

1. **God's prophet Elisha showed kindness to a woman whose son had died. God will help us look for ways to be kind to others and care for them. Let's try doing that during our game today!**
2. Group kids into teams of six to eight. Teams are to line up single-file about 5' from the container. Give each student an index card. Give the first student on each team a ball or beanbag.
3. Stand near the container with the marker in your hand. Students from each team are to take turns tossing the ball or beanbag into the container. Each time a student gets the ball or beanbag into the container, print one letter of the word *kindness* on his or her index card.

4. When a student gets all the letters for the word, he or she continues taking turns, giving any letters scored to the next person in line. Continue until all students have *kindness* written on their cards.

Discussion Questions

1. **In this game, how did we show kindness?** (gave letters to others)
2. **What are some ways to be kind to others and care about them?** (ask someone to play with you if he or she is looking lonely, share with others, help someone or get help for someone who needs it, use kind words when you speak to others)
3. Have a volunteer read Matthew 5:7 aloud. **Jesus taught it is good to show mercy or compassion to others. What can you do to discover ways to show mercy to others?** (pray and ask God to help me think of kind things to do, take more time to notice the people around me instead of just thinking about myself)

Memory Moves

Bible Focus ▸ John 15:12

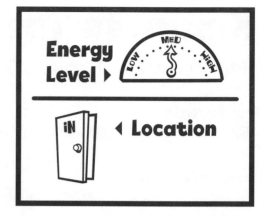

Materials
Bibles, whiteboard, dry-erase marker

Preparation
Print the words of John 15:12 on the board.

Lead the Game

1. **We can follow Jesus' example of showing love by being loving to people whom others ignore. Let's play a game that reminds us to show love to others!**

2. Ask a volunteer to read John 15:12 aloud. **Jesus spoke these words. What did Jesus tell us to do?** (to love others as Jesus has loved us) Ask kids to say the verse together.

3. Have students stand in a circle. In order around the circle, assign each student a word from the verse for which to create a motion. Each student is to think of and practice a simple motion for his or her word.

4. To begin, the student with the first word of the verse says his or her word while doing the motion he or she created. The next student says the first word while doing the first student's motion and then says his or her own word while doing a motion. Continue around the circle in that manner until the entire verse is recited with motions. Then ask everyone to try saying the entire verse with motions.

Discussion Questions

1. **What kinds of people does Jesus love?** (every kind, all people)
2. **In what ways did Jesus show love to people when He was on earth?** (talked to them, helped them with their problems, cared for them, fed them) **What can we do to follow Jesus' examples of loving people?**
3. **Where are some places kids your age get ignored?** (at school on the playground, at a friend's house) **What are some ways you can show love to these kids?** (talk to them, invite them to play a game with you, share something with them)

Name Game

Bible Focus ▶ Genesis 1:26–27; 2:7, 15–23

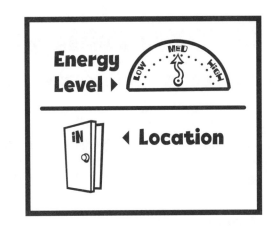

Materials
whiteboard, dry-erase marker

Game Tip
Print "Vowel = Jump" and "Consonant = Squat" on the board for students to refer to during the game.

Lead the Game

1. **God created us to love Him and love each other. One way to love and care for others is to learn their names. Let's play a fun game with everyone's name!**

2. Group students into teams of six to eight students each. Teams should line up in single-file lines, leaving at least 4' between each team.

3. **In our game today, each of you will take a turn to call out the letters of your name to your team. When you say a vowel—A, E, I, O, U— your team members are to jump up. When you say a consonant— any of the other letters—your team members are to squat down. Let's practice with my first name.** Call out the letters of your first name; all students should jump up or squat down according to the letters called.

4. At your signal, the first student on each team begins calling out the letters of his or her first name, while the other students on the team jump up or squat down according to the letter called. When the first student is done, the second team member calls out the letters of his or her name with teammates responding as above. Each team continues the process as quickly as possible, sitting down as soon as all members of the team have spelled out their names. Have the first team to finish answer one of the discussion questions. As time allows, have kids form new teams and play again.

Discussion Questions

1. **Why should we show love to others?** (The Bible says the most important things we can do are to love God and love others.)

2. **What are some ways we can show love to others?**

Overflowing Love

Bible Focus ▶ 1 Thessalonians 3:12

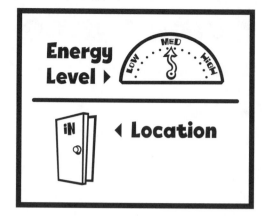

Materials
Bibles, dried beans, measuring cup, 2 of each of the following: large plastic bowls, spoons, large paper cups, shallow baking pans (or boxes)

Preparation
Pour at least three cups of beans into each plastic bowl. Place the plastic bowls and spoons on one side of the playing area. Put the paper cups in shallow pans or boxes and place them on the opposite side of the playing area.

Lead the Game
1. **Showing love means doing good things for others without expecting anything in return. Let's play a game about a Bible verse that tells us how God helps us to show love!**
2. Divide the class into two teams. Teams are to line up in single-file lines next to the spoons. Have a volunteer read 1 Thessalonians 3:12 aloud. **What does this verse say God will do?** ("make your love increase and overflow") **You'll know your love is overflowing when you show love and kindness to others without even thinking about what they might do for you in return.**
3. **In this game, see how long it takes to make your team's cup overflow with beans.** At your signal, the first student on each team takes a spoonful of beans, walks quickly to his or her team's cup, drops in the beans, returns to the team, and hands the spoon to the next player. Any spilled beans need to be picked up. The next student in each line repeats action. Relay continues until both teams have made their cups overflow with beans and the beans spill into the pan or box. Repeat as time allows, asking the Discussion Questions below between rounds.

Discussion Questions
1. **When are some times it's easy to show love to others?** (when others have been kind to us) **When might it be hard to show love to others?** (when we're angry or upset)
2. **What can we do when we don't feel like showing love?** (ask God to help our love increase and overflow, remember God's love for us)
3. **What are some ways you could let kindness overflow with your family? Your friends at school? Someone you dislike? What good things might happen?**

Red-Carpet Crossing

Bible Focus ▶ Genesis 13:1–9; Romans 12:18

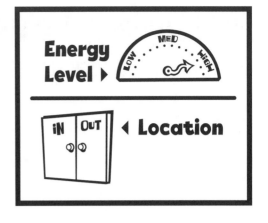

Materials
Bibles, 2 sheets of red construction paper for each pair of students

Lead the Game
1. **Abram made peace with his nephew Lot by letting him choose which land to live in. Putting others first can also help us to be peacemakers. Let's practice putting others first by playing a game where we must help others!**
2. **Red carpets are often laid down for important people to walk on as they enter buildings. When we treat someone as being important or special, it's like we are giving that person the "red-carpet treatment." In this game, we'll practice putting each other first by giving each other the red-carpet treatment with these papers.**

3. Have kids form pairs and stand on one side of the classroom. They should decide which student in each pair will be the helper. Give each pair two sheets of red construction paper. At your signal, each helper lays down a sheet of paper for his or her partner to step on. The helper places the next paper one step away, and the partner moves to that paper. The helper picks up the first sheet and then places it in front of his or her partner. Pairs should move in this manner to the opposite side of the playing area and then race back to their starting positions. Ask the winning pair to answer one of the discussion questions.
4. Then have kids switch roles and repeat the game. (You could replace paper that was torn.)

Option
If there is not enough room for all pairs to play at the same time, have them form teams of up to six pairs each. Teams complete the game in relay fashion, one pair from each team going at a time.

Discussion Questions
1. **How did you put others first in this game?** (moved the paper for my partner)
2. Have a volunteer Romans 12:18 aloud. **What are some ways you can live at peace with others by putting them first?** (let my sister have the last cookie, let a classmate have the first turn at the computer)
3. **How does putting others first help keep the peace?** (keeps fights from starting, shows we care about the other person)

Relaying Love

Bible Focus ▶ Luke 10:25–37

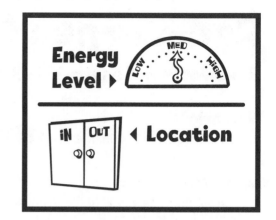

Energy Level ▶

Location ▶

Materials
index cards, marker

Preparation
Print each of these kinds of people on separate index cards: baby, old person, basketball player, soccer player, toddler, movie star, teenager, race car driver, juggler.

Lead the Game
1. **In Bible times, Jewish and Samaritan people didn't get along. Jesus told a story about a Samaritan man who helped a Jewish man who had been robbed and beaten. Loving God means loving all kinds of people. We're going to play a game in which we need different kinds of people in order to play the game!**
2. Group kids into two equal teams. Teams are to line up on one side of an open area in your classroom. You should stand between the two teams.
3. At your signal, the first student in each team runs to you. Show each student one of the cards you prepared. The students return to their teams and then move across the room and back as though they were (basketball players). Students should continue taking turns until all kids on each team have had a turn. Play as many rounds of the game as time permits.

Option
Place a chair or cone on the opposite side of the room from each team. Students must move around the chair or cone to complete the relay.

Discussion Questions
1. **What kinds of people were needed to play this game?** (toddler, basketball player)
2. **One way to love God is to show His love to all kinds of people. How can you show love to people who are different from you?** (talk to kids I don't usually play with, ask a new person to sit with me and my friends at lunch, don't join in with others who are making fun of someone else)
3. **Why does God want us to love others?** (God made and loves all people. Each person is important to God.)

Big Book of Bible Games
for Elementary Kids
© David C Cook. Permission granted to photocopy for ministry purposes only.

Three-Legged Race

Bible Focus ▶ 2 Kings 5

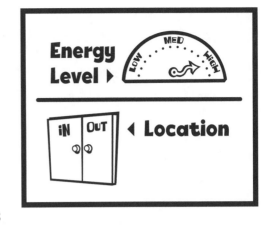

Energy Level ▶ LOW MED HIGH

iN OUT ◀ Location

Materials
scarves (or fabric strips) at least 21" in length (1 per pair of kids)

Lead the Game
1. **The prophet Elisha helped an army commander by healing him of leprosy. Helping others is something we can do to show God's love to others. Let's play a game in which you need to help your partner!**
2. Group students into pairs. Help pairs of students to tie their inside legs together with a scarf or fabric strip (see sketch). Let kids walk around an open playing area in your classroom or outdoors. **What makes it hard to move quickly? What can you do to make it easier?**
3. Ask pairs to stand on one side of open playing area in your classroom or outdoors. At your signal, pairs are to race to the other side of the playing area. Repeat the race several times or as time and interest permit.

Discussion Questions
1. **What are some other games in which the players need to help their teammates?** (soccer, volleyball) **How do players in these games help each other?**
2. **What are some ways that others have helped you?**
3. **What are some ways that you can help someone younger than you? Older than you?**

Wall-Building Relay

Bible Focus ▸ Nehemiah 1–4; 6:15–16;
1 Thessalonians 5:11

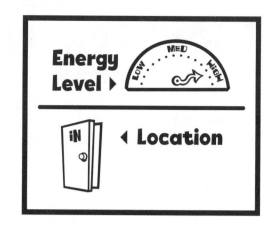

Energy Level ▸

◀ Location

Materials
Bibles, 2 large sheets of paper, masking tape, self-stick notes, timer

Preparation
Tape two large sheets of paper on one wall of the room, leaving some space between the two papers. Place a large stack of self-stick notes next to each paper.

Lead the Game

1. **The good news about being in God's family is that we can encourage one another to love and obey God and to do His work! That's what happened when Nehemiah and some others in Israel worked together to rebuild the wall around Jerusalem. Let's work together to build our own wall!**
2. Group students into two teams. Teams are to line up on the opposite side of the playing area from the sheets of paper.
3. At your signal, start the timer and send the first student on each team to his or her team's paper. Each student should stick a self-stick note onto the bottom part of the paper, then return to his or her team. The next student in line repeats the action. Students on each team continue taking turns building their team's wall. Tell students to encourage each other as they build their walls.
4. After several minutes, call time and compare the walls. The team with the largest wall can answer one of the discussion questions. Then ask the other discussion questions. If time allows, turn papers over for students to play the game again.

Option
Instead of using self-stick notes, students can build walls by taping newspapers to long lengths of roll paper.

Discussion Questions
1. **Why is it important to encourage other people?** (It's a way to follow God's command to love one another. Everyone needs encouragment.) Have a volunteer read 1 Thessalonians 5:11 aloud.
2. **What are some things you could do or say to encourage others?** (pray for them, offer to help them, listen to them, point out good things that they're doing)

Life Application Games

Telling Others about Jesus

Fast Phrase

Bible Focus ▶ Matthew 3; John 1:29–34

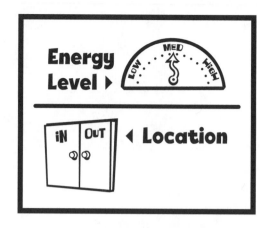

Lead the Game

1. **John the Baptist's announcement about Jesus helped everyone know Jesus is the Savior. We're going to play a game to announce this same great news!**

2. Choose a volunteer to be the announcer. At your signal, students should begin walking around the room. When the announcer says, "Hear this! Hear this!" students should stop walking, spin around, and sit down on the floor as quickly as they can. The first student to sit down tells something he or she knows about Jesus or answers one of the questions below. Then that student becomes the new announcer. Keep playing as time and interest allow. (If the first student to be seated has already been the announcer, he or she can choose someone who hasn't yet had a turn to be the announcer.)

Option

Encourage the announcer to say, "Hear this! Hear this!" in an attention-grabbing way: loudly, clapping on each syllable, and so forth.

Game Tip

If it's difficult to determine who sits first, call out another criteria (student wearing the most blue, whose birthday is closest, most letters in last name).

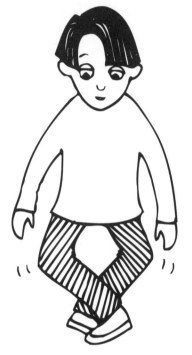

Discussion Questions

1. **Some people learned that Jesus is the Savior by hearing John's announcement or by seeing Jesus being baptized. What are some ways you've learned that Jesus is God's Son, the Savior?**

2. **What does it mean to say Jesus is the Savior?** (Jesus saves us from the punishment we deserve for our sins.)

3. **How might you "announce" that Jesus is God's Son, the Savior?** (tell a friend why I celebrate Christmas, ask a friend to come to church, pray before eating)

He's Alive! Relay

Bible Focus ▸ Matthew 28:1–10; Mark 16:1–11;
Luke 24:1–12; John 20

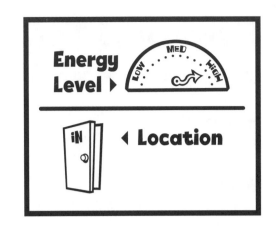

Energy Level ▸

iN ◂ Location

Materials
large sheets of white and brown (or gray) paper, scissors,
black markers (Optional: self-stick notes, pencils)

Preparation
Cut paper into rock shapes, creating a paper rock for every four to six students.
Place paper rocks on one side of the playing area. Place a black marker
next to each paper rock.

Lead the Game
1. **When Mary Magdalene went to Jesus' tomb,
   what did she find?** (The stone had been rolled
   back and the tomb was empty.) **Mary, Peter,
   and John discovered the tomb was empty
   because Jesus had risen from the dead and
   was alive! What did they all do next?** (They told
   everyone that Jesus had risen!)

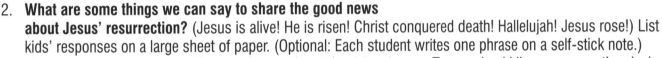

2. **What are some things we can say to share the good news
   about Jesus' resurrection?** (Jesus is alive! He is risen! Christ conquered death! Hallelujah! Jesus rose!) List
   kids' responses on a large sheet of paper. (Optional: Each student writes one phrase on a self-stick note.)
3. Group students into teams of four to six, creating at least two teams. Teams should line up across the playing
   area from the paper rocks. At your signal, the first student from each team runs to his or her team's paper rock
   and writes one good news phrase on the rock. The student calls out the phrase and returns to his or her line,
   tagging the next student. The next student repeats the action. (Optional: Students stick self-stick notes on the
   rock.) Tell kids that they can refer to the list of responses during the relay as needed. The relay continues until
   all kids have had a turn. Repeat the relay as time permits.

Discussion Questions
1. **What does Jesus' death and resurrection mean for us?** (Jesus' resurrection shows He has power over
   death. Jesus died on the cross to take away our sins. His resurrection means Christians will live with Him in
   heaven forever.)
2. **With whom can you share this good news?**

Hop and Tell

Bible Focus ▶ Acts 14:8–20

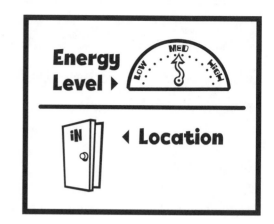

Energy Level ▶

iN ◀ Location

Materials
markers, roll paper, masking tape

Preparation
On a length of roll paper, draw one large snail-shaped spiral for every five students. Divide each spiral into a dozen spaces, marking the center circle "Rest" (see sketch). Tape each paper spiral to the floor.

Lead the Game
1. **The apostles Paul and Barnabas healed people and preached about Jesus wherever they went. To help others learn about God, we can also tell about the great and wonderful things Jesus has done. In our game today, we'll practice telling some of those great and wonderful things!**
2. Gather students into groups of five. Tell each group to stand at one of the snail-shaped spirals.
3. The first student in each group hops on one foot all the way around the spiral to the "Rest" circle, where she can rest on both feet before turning and hopping back on one foot. If he or she hops back and forth without hopping on any lines or putting both feet down (except in the "Rest" circle), that student writes in one of the spaces a great and wonderful thing God has done. The next student repeats the action, and if he or she is successful, that student writes in another space a great and wonderful thing God has done. Continue the game until all kids have written something or as time allows.

Option
Rather than preparing snail-shaped spirals ahead of time, allow groups to create their own game paths in class. Suggest curved or zigzag path options.

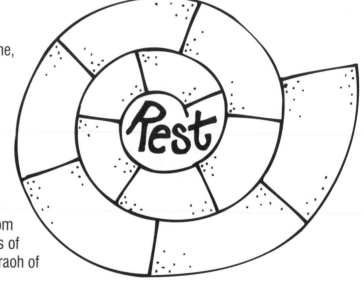

Discussion Questions
1. **What are some of the great and wonderful things God has done that you wrote?**
2. **What are some more great things God has done that you have heard about or read in the Bible?** (created the world, saved Noah and the animals from the flood, sent Jesus to us, pushed back the waters of the Red Sea so the Israelites could escape the Pharaoh of Egypt)
3. **What are some great things God has done for you or other people you know?** (took the punishment for our sins, answers prayers, shows love)

Secret Card Pass

Bible Focus ▸ Matthew 3:13–17;
Mark 1:4–11; John 1:29–34

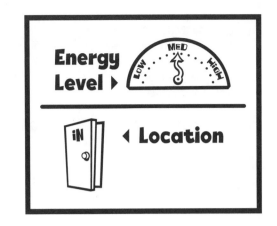

Energy Level ▸

Location ▸

Materials
small index cards, marker

Lead the Game

1. **When Jesus was baptized, God announced from heaven that Jesus is His Son. Let's play a game to make some other announcements about Jesus!**

2. **What are some true statements about Jesus?** (Jesus is God's Son. Jesus died and rose again. Jesus came to earth and was born as a baby. Jesus healed people. Jesus did miracles.) List the statements on separate small index cards.

3. Students should stand in a circle (shoulder-to-shoulder, if possible) to play a game similar to Button, Button, Who's Got the Button? Choose one student to be "It." "It" stands in the middle of the circle with eyes closed.

4. Give one of the index cards to a student in the circle. "It" opens his or her eyes. At your signal, students are to pass the card around the circle behind their backs, trying to keep "It" from seeing who has the card. After 15 to 20 seconds, signal students to stop passing the card. "It" tries to identify who has the card. After "It" guesses or after two tries, the student holding the card reads aloud the announcement about Jesus. (Give help with reading as needed.) Choose a new volunteer and repeat the game with a different index card.

Options
1. Play music while students pass the card.
2. If you have a large group of students, kids could pass more than one index card at a time.

Discussion Questions
1. **God spoke from heaven to tell everyone that Jesus is His Son. What are some ways people make announcements today?** (email, social media, website, letter or flier, radio, TV)
2. **What did Jesus do as God's Son?** (Jesus died to save all people from their sins. He healed people. He cared for the sick and the poor. He taught people how to love others.)
3. **How can we help people learn that Jesus is God's Son?** (invite them to church services, tell them stories about Jesus)

Sprint to Share Jesus

Bible Focus ▶ Acts 26; 1 Peter 3:15

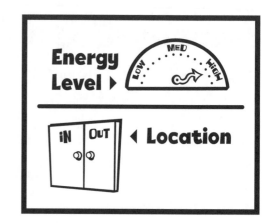

Energy Level ▶

iN OUT ◀ Location

Materials
Bibles, masking tape, 1 spoon for every 6 to 8 students, dry beans

Preparation
Make a masking-tape line on one side of an open playing area.

Lead the Game

1. **The apostle Paul told everyone he could about Jesus. When he was in prison, Paul told about Jesus. And when Paul had the opportunity to speak to important leaders, he told them about Jesus too. Just like Paul, it's important for us to keep on telling people about Jesus, looking for ways to share God's love with others in every situation. In our game today, we're going to discuss different ways to share God's love!**

2. Group students into teams of six to eight. Teams should line up in single-file lines opposite the masking-tape line. Hand a spoon to the first student on each team. Place five or six beans on each spoon.

3. At your signal, the first student from each team moves across the playing area to the masking-tape line. Students may use only one hand to hold the spoon, trying not to drop any beans. If they spill some beans, kids are to put the spilled beans back on the spoons before continuing. Once they have crossed the line, students turn around and return to their teams. Then kids pass the spoons to the next players who continue in the same manner until all team members have had a turn.

4. Have the first team to finish tell a situation when kids could tell others about God and share His love. When finished playing, ask the discussion questions.

Discussion Questions

1. **What are some ways to share God's love at home? In your neighborhood?**
2. Have a volunteer read 1 Peter 3:15 aloud. **Why is it important that when you tell someone about God's love, you also treat them with love and kindness?**
3. **What are some things you could tell others when they ask you about God?** (Jesus loves everyone, including them. God hears and answers prayers.)

Big Book of Bible Games for Elementary Kids

W-I-T-N-E-S-S

Bible Focus ▶ Acts 1:8

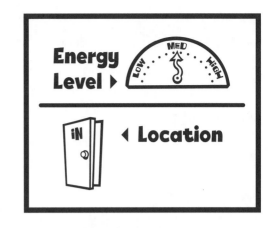

Materials
Bibles, whiteboard, dry-erase marker, masking tape, soft ball, large container

Preparation
Draw a line down the center of the board. Print "Team 1" on one side and "Team 2" on the other.

Lead the Game

1. **Jesus' disciples witnessed, or saw, the miracles Jesus did. The miracles showed everyone that Jesus is God's Son. So when the disciples went out and "witnessed," they were telling others about Jesus.** Divide the class into two teams. Play a basketball-type game similar to H-O-R-S-E. Teams take turns attempting to toss the ball into a container. Each time the ball lands in the container, a student from that team writes a letter of the word *witness* on its side of the board.
2. When a team completes the word, have that team answer a discussion question.
3. Mix up the teams, and continue playing as time permits.

Option
In each round, use a different method to divide the group into teams. Try one or more of the following: students line up in alphabetical order according to the first letter of first names. Put every other student on team 2 (the others are team 1). Students group themselves by a color on their clothes or the kind of shoes they are wearing. Students line up by birthday months, starting with January.

Discussion Questions
1. **Why do you want to be part of God's family?** You may want to tell your own reasons for becoming a Christian before asking students to do so.
2. Have a volunteer read Acts 1:8 aloud. **Who does God give us so we can tell others about Jesus?** (the Holy Spirit)
3. **What are some ways you can tell others about Jesus?**

Witness Walkabout

Bible Focus ▸ Acts 28:17–31

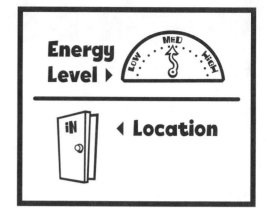

Energy Level ▸

iN ◂ Location

Materials

children's music from your collection, music player, construction paper, markers, timer

Lead the Game

1. **Paul wanted to go to Rome so he could tell the Roman people about Jesus. The book of Acts says Paul did go to Rome and he spent two years there writing and telling others about Jesus.** Distribute construction paper to students. **What kinds of people could you talk to about Jesus?** (parents, siblings, neighbors, grandparents, kids at school) As students name types of people, have kids take turns writing names on separate sheets of construction paper. For your own reference, you can make a list on a sheet of paper. Continue printing specific types of people on papers until there is a paper for each student. **What are some of the ways we can tell others about Jesus?** (ask a friend to watch a video about Jesus with you, answer their questions about Jesus, tell what you have learned from reading the Bible or from Sunday school, give them a Bible or Bible story book)

2. Lead the kids in a game similar to Cakewalk. Place the people papers in a circle on the floor. Play music for 15 to 20 seconds as students move around the circle. When the music stops, each student is to stand on the paper that is closest to him or her. Name one of the people from your list. The student standing on that paper is to say something about Jesus that he or she can tell that person. If a student needs help thinking of things to tell others, ask a discussion question.

Discussion Questions

1. **Who is Jesus? What did He do for all people? Why is that important? What is the most important thing you know about Jesus?**
2. **When did you first learn about Jesus? Who talked to you about Jesus?**
3. **What are some things you could tell others if they asked you about Jesus?** (Jesus loves you. Jesus died on the cross so your sins could be forgiven. Jesus loves everyone and wants everyone to believe in Him.)

Recreational Games

All Together Now

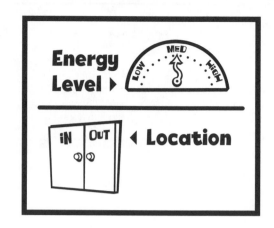

Materials
chalk (or masking tape or rope), several balloons

Preparation
On the ground or floor, make a start and finish line with chalk, masking tape, or rope, approximately 20 yards apart. Inflate the balloons.

Lead the Game
1. Divide the group into two teams. Each team should stand behind the starting line and make a tight circle with their hands extended into the middle. Each team member grabs a hand or two of other team members. The teacher places a balloon on the top of each team's grasped hands (see sketch).
2. When the teacher says, "Go!" each team is to run to the finish line and back keeping the balloon on top of their grasped hands. It is against the rules to wedge the balloon between arms. If a team drops the balloon, that team must start over. The first team to complete the race wins.

Option
For a greater challenge, increase the number of balloons for each relay run.

A-MAZE-ing Art

Materials
outdoor area with asphalt (or concrete) surface, sidewalk chalk in various colors

Preparation
Secure the outside area before the game.

Energy Level ▶

OUT ◀ Location

Lead the Game
1. Divide the group into teams of three or four players. Give each team chalk in a variety of colors.
2. Each team is to use the chalk to draw a complicated maze on the ground. First, players should draw a simple outline of the path. Then they can fill in the outline with details, such as dead-ends and obstacles. When the mazes are complete, teams should take turns trying to walk through each other's mazes.

Option
If outdoor space is not available, teams can use markers to draw mazes on paper. When finished, teams can trade papers and try to solve each other's mazes.

Bail Out!

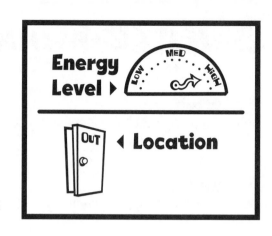

OUT ◀ Location

Materials
inflatable 2-person (or 3-person) raft (or small wading pool), water; 2 (or 3) plastic gallon jugs, craft knife, sidewalk chalk (or rope)

Preparation
In an outdoor area, fill a raft or wading pool with water. Cut off the neck of each milk jug to enlarge the opening (see sketch a). Use sidewalk chalk or rope to make a starting line about 20' from the raft. Make a finish line about 10' beyond the raft.

Lead the Game
Does anyone know what SOS means? (save our ship) **Our "ship" is full of water! To save it, we'll have to bail it out.** Divide the group into two or three equally numbered teams. Teams are to line up behind the starting line. Give the first player on each team a milk jug. At your signal, the first player on each team carries a milk jug to the raft, fills the jug with water, and runs to the finish line. The player then flings the water out past the finish line and runs back to give the empty jug to the next player. The first team to have all players complete the relay wins.

Game Tip
Explain how it's become common for us to connect SOS to the phrase "Save Our Ship," but actually SOS doesn't stand for anything! It was adopted in 1906 as an international distress signal, because Morse code for SOS (• • • — — — • • •) is easy to send by telegraph and unlikely to be misinterpreted.

a.  Cut.

b.

Beach Bowling

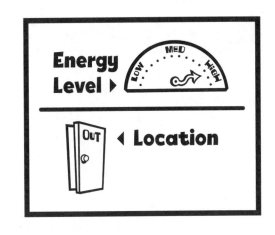

Energy Level ▶

OUT ◀ Location

Materials
several bags of sand (or chalk or rope), tape measure, 2 buckets, water, 2 soft balls, 2 pieces of paper, 2 pencils, four 16-oz. plastic drinking cups (Optional: 2 plastic trash bags)

Preparation
Pour two piles of moistened sand on the pavement or grass. (Optonal: Pour sand on top of plastic trash bags for easy clean up.) Set buckets full of water close to the sand piles for additional dampening, as needed. Use chalk or rope to make a line about 10' from each pile of sand (see sketch a).

Lead the Game
1. Divide the group into two equal teams. Using plastic cups, two members of each team are to mold sand into six sand bowling pins (see sketch b). These two students will act as ball retrievers and pin setters and stand near the bowling pins.
2. The other members of each team should line up behind the line. The first player on each team rolls a soft ball, trying to knock down as many sand pins as possible. Teams should write down the number of sand pins knocked down. Then the pin setters rebuild the pins. The first player then replaces one pin setter, who goes to the end of the team's line. Then the second player on each team bowls, and then replaces the other pin setter. This continues until each player has had a turn to bowl. Teams should total their points. The team with the highest score wins.

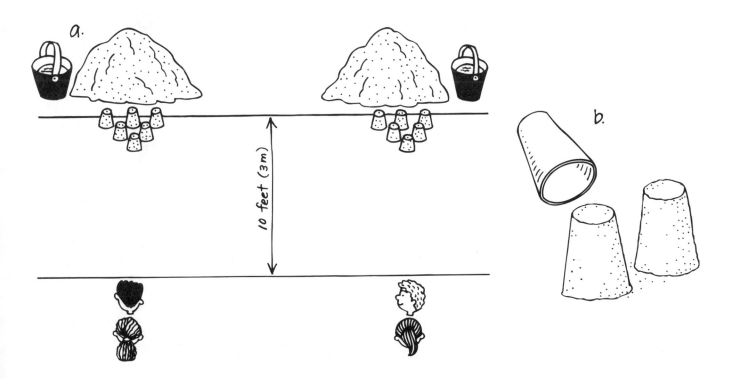

a.

10 feet (3m)

b.

Beach-Fun Relay

Energy Level ▶ LOW MED HIGH

OUT ◀ Location

Materials

4 laundry baskets (or boxes), water, chalk (or rope), beach equipment (boogie board, kickboard, sand shovel, snorkeling mask, swim fins, etc.), tape measure, water balloons (at least 2 per student)

Preparation

Fill water balloons with water and tie to secure. Place an equal number of water balloons into two baskets or boxes. Mark a starting line with chalk or rope. Place an empty basket or box for each team on the starting line. Approximately 15' away, place a water balloon basket or box for each team (see sketch).

Lead the Game

1. Divide the group into two equal teams. Let each student select one item of beach equipment to use to transport the water balloons.

2. At your signal, the first player on each team races to his or her team's basket of balloons. The player selects a water balloon and then transports it back to the team's empty box using the beach equipment. (Examples: carry the balloon on a kick board, carry the balloon while wearing swim fins, carry the balloon with a sand shovel) If a water balloon breaks in transit, the player may go back to the balloon box, select another water balloon, and try again. (You may wish to set a limit of two tries for each player.) Once the team member returns, the next player races to retrieve a balloon. The team with the most balloons in their box wins.

Big Book of Bible Games
for Elementary Kids
© David C Cook. Permission granted to photocopy for ministry purposes only.

Crazy Beach Ball

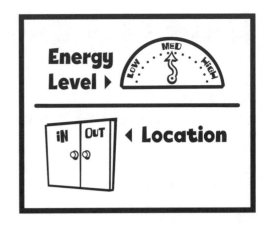

iN OUT ◀ Location

Materials
chalk (or masking tape), tape measure, rope (or volleyball net), 2 poles secured in ground or in stands, inflated beach ball

Preparation
Use chalk or tape to mark a volleyball court (20' x 30') on the floor, pavement, or grass. Stretch the rope or the volleyball net between poles, approximately 4' from the ground (see sketch).

Lead the Game
The game is played similar to volleyball. Each team may have up to nine players (three rows of three players). To start each set, the server tosses the ball over the net from the front row. The ball may be hit with any part of the body above the waist. The ball is allowed to hit the ground once on each side before it is returned over the net. If the ball hits the ground twice before being returned, the opposing team scores a point regardless of which side served. The ball may be hit up to five times before it must go over the net. The ball may not be held. If a team hits the ball out of bounds, the opposite team scores one point. The first team to get 15 points wins.

20 feet (6m)

30 feet (9m)

Hold the Ropes

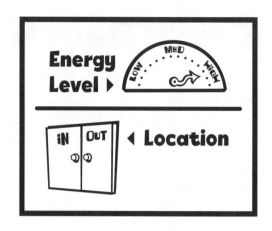

Energy Level ▶ LOW MED HIGH

iN OUT ◀ Location

Materials
8 chairs, inflated balloon (1 per team, plus a few extras), a 6' rope for each team

Preparation
Place four chairs in a line along one end of the playing area and four chairs in a line on the opposite side at least 40' apart.

Lead the Game
1. Divide the group into four teams. Each team forms a line behind a chair. The first player in each line is given a balloon and a rope. When you shout, "Hold the ropes!" the first player on each team holds the balloon and the rope and runs around a chair at the opposite side, returning to his or her team. The first player hands the balloon to the second player. Then the first and second players, both holding the rope, run around the chair and back (see sketch).
2. The relay continues until the entire team is holding the rope, with the last player holding the balloon, as they run around the chair and back. If a player lets go of the rope or drops the balloon, the team has to return to the starting place and begin again. The first team to complete the relay wins.

Hoop-Crash Race

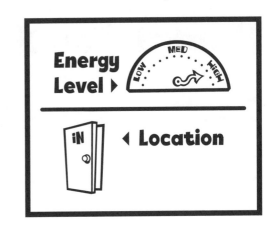
Energy Level ▶ LOW · MED · HIGH

iN ◀ Location

Materials
obstacles to get in the way of hoops (chairs, books, boxes, etc.), masking tape, sidewalk chalk (or rope), 2 Hula-Hoops

Preparation
Create two similar obstacle courses that will provide a challenge rolling a hoop through. Mark a starting line for two teams to play side-by-side.

Lead the Game
Divide the group into two teams. Each team is to line up behind the starting line. The first player on each team places the hoop upright and rolls it through the obstacle course, then returns to tag the next player. If the hoop falls over, the player stands it up and continues on. The first team to have all its players complete the relay wins.

Option
For an additional challenge, players could use rulers to push the hoop through the course.

Human Foosball

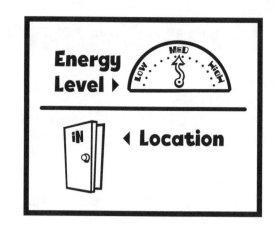

Materials
masking tape, chairs, tennis ball (or soft foam ball)

Preparation
Tear off masking-tape strips (two per student). Position chairs as shown in the sketch.

Lead the Game
1. Divide the group into two teams. Position students as shown in the sketch, each team facing away from its respective goalie. Students should stand at least an arm's length from each other. Give each student two strips of masking tape. Students on one team should make masking-tape Xs on the floor to mark their positions. Students on the other team should make masking-tape Ls on the floor.
2. Gently roll the ball toward the middle of the playing area. Students try to kick the ball toward their team's goal, each student keeping at least one foot on his or her masking-tape mark at all times. Kids are not allowed to touch the ball with their hands.
3. Students should continue kicking the ball until a goal is scored. (Note: Goalies can only use their feet to defend a goal.) Begin again by giving the ball to a player from the team that did not score.

Options
1. Play outside with a soccer ball or playground ball, and use chalk to mark students' positions.
2. Players may be seated on chairs instead of standing on masking-tape marks.
3. If you have an uneven number of students, ask a volunteer to help you retrieve balls that roll out of the playing area. Rotate the volunteer into the game after each goal is scored.

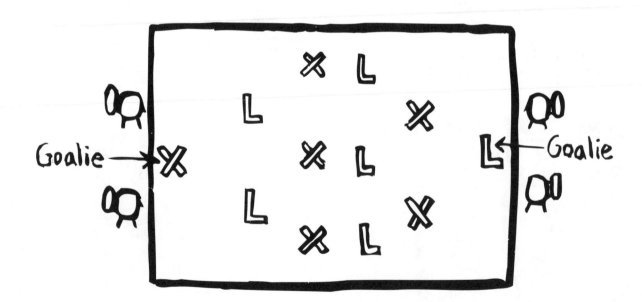

Big Book of Bible Games
for Elementary Kids

Mass Transit

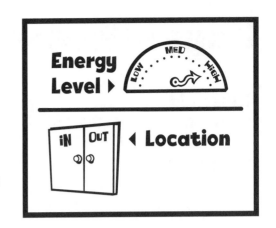
Materials
chalk, 4 large appliance boxes, craft knife, whistle

Preparation
Using chalk, draw four starting lines on opposite sides of an open area at least 20 yards square. Cut out two sides of each box (see sketch).

Lead the Game
1. Divide the group into four teams. Each team is to choose a name for its box for the race. Have the teams gather at a starting line, and place a box by each starting line. When you blow the whistle, all team members get inside the box, lift the box, and run to the opposite side of the playing area.
2. At the opposite side, all team members must get out of the box, run around it five times, give a high-five to each team member, and get back in the box. Then the team runs back to its place. The first team to reach its starting place wins.

Oops! Water Ball

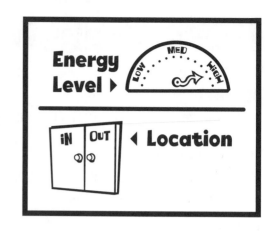

Energy Level ▶ LOW MED HIGH

iN OUT ◀ Location

Materials
volleyball net (or rope and posts); sheets, blankets, or plastic sheeting; clothespins; water balloons; water

Preparation
Set up the volleyball net in a large outdoor area. Use clothespins to attach sheets, blankets, or plastic sheeting across the entire width of the net. Teams should not be able to see each other (except for feet). Fill balloons with a small amount of water and tie to secure.

Lead the Game
Divide the group into two equal teams. Begin play with only one water balloon. Teams are to toss the water balloon back and forth across the net, trying to catch it and return it without breaking it. When the balloon bursts, the team who failed to catch it must shout, "Oops, ball!" and the other team scores a point. Replace the burst balloon with two balloons (one for each side) and continue play. Add two balloons for each one that breaks. For added fun, poke a pinhole in some of the balloons so that players are squirted as they play.

Option
For a drier or indoor version, use foam-type balls instead of water balloons.

Reverse Baseball

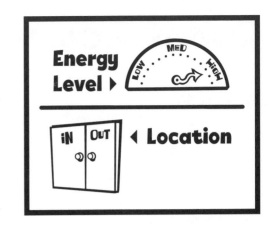

Energy Level ▶

Location ▶

Materials

4 bases, traffic cones (or other large markers), rubber kickball, measuring tape

Preparation

Set up bases, traffic cones, or markers in a diamond shape as in regular kickball. Bases should be about 20' apart.

Lead the Game

Divide the group into two teams. Explain that the game is played like regular kickball, but in this "reverse universe," players must run around the bases backwards (going to third base first). Runners must be tagged with the ball to be out. If a runner reaches home base without being tagged, his or her team gets one point. Teams take turns after three outs.

Option

Increase the challenge by having players run the bases facing backwards as well.

home base

Robot Action

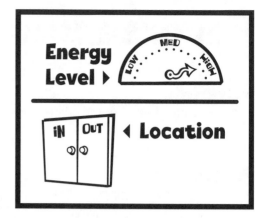

Energy Level ▶

◀ Location

Materials

chalk (or rope), 2 medium-sized boxes large enough to fit over children's heads, craft knife, markers and/or paint, old newspaper (or recycled paper), 2 wastebaskets (or cans), measuring tape, 2 sets of knee and elbow guards, 2 brooms

Preparation

Use chalk or rope to mark a starting line. Use a craft knife to cut two large eye circles out of each box. Use markers and/or paint to decorate each box to look like a robot's head. Crumple newspaper to make medium-sized trash balls—one for each player. Place the trash balls in one big pile near the starting line. Place wastebaskets about 20 to 30 feet from the starting line. Wastebaskets will serve as the finish line.

Lead the Game

Divide the class into two teams and have the teams line up behind the starting line. The first players on each team puts guards on their knees and elbows and a robot box over their heads. Give both players a broom. Each "robot" is to sweep one trash ball to the finish line, bend over to place the ball in the wastepaper basket, and race back to tag the next player. The next player in line puts on the robot gear and continues the race in relay fashion. The first team to have all players dispose of a trash ball and return to the starting line wins.

shin guards

Rocket Launch

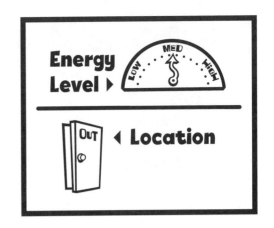

Materials
volleyball net (or rope), 2 sturdy chairs, water balloons, water, 4 small blankets (or sheets)

Preparation
Tie the volleyball net or rope across two chairs. Fill several water balloons with water and tie to secure.

Lead the Game
Divide the group into four teams of at least four players each, and place two teams on either side of the net. Give a blanket or sheet to each team. Team members are to stretch the blanket or sheet taut. Choose one side of the net to make the first launch. Place water balloons in the center of both teams' blankets or sheets. Team members work together to "rocket" their balloons over the net (see sketch). To improve teamwork, encourage teams to count backwards to launch saying, "3-2-1, launch!" Receiving teams try to catch the rockets on their blankets. Play continues back and forth across the net. (Note: diagonal shots are allowed and will add to the fun!) Teams score one point every time the receiving team fails to catch the rocket on their blanket or sheet. Replace burst rockets with new ones. For fun, poke a pinhole in one of the water balloons so children get squirted as they play.

Option
For an indoor version of this game, use beanbags instead of water balloons.

Rowboat Race

Materials
rope, tape measure

Preparation
On a grassy area, use the rope to make a starting line and finish line about 15' apart.

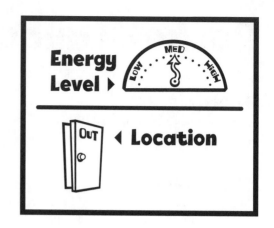

Energy Level ▶

Out ◀ Location

Lead the Game
1. Divide the group into pairs. Each partner A sits on the starting line with legs extended straight out and knees together. Each partner B sits facing partner A with soles of shoes touching. Partner B has knees bent and clasps hands of partner A (see sketch a).
2. To move, partner B pulls partner A until knees are in a bent position (see sketch b). Then partner B pushes back to straighten his or her legs and pushes partner B's legs back into a bent position (see sketch d). This pushing and pulling motion "rows" players along, about a yard at a time. Give each pair a few minutes to practice rowing. Then say, **"Rowing positions!"** Partners position themselves behind the starting line. When you say, "Go!" the pairs begin rowing to the finish line. The pair that reaches the finish line first wins. If a pair breaks apart, they must stop and get into the rowing position before they begin rowing again.

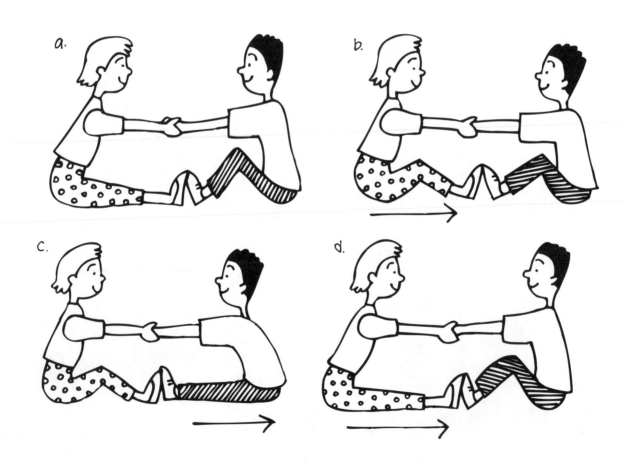

Shoot the Rapids

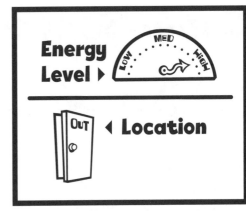

Energy Level ▶

◀ Location

Materials
2 Slip 'N Slides (or 24' x 20' lengths of heavy, plastic sheeting), 2 garden hoses and faucets, 2 lengths of rope 5' long, 2 inner tubes (or small inflatable rafts), several towels

Preparation
Set up the Slip 'N Slides or plastic sheeting lengths on a grassy area, parallel to each other. Attach a hose to each Slip 'N Slide or have a helper hold the hose over the plastic sheeting during the game. Tie a rope to each inner tube or raft and place at one end of each water slide.

Lead the Game
1. Have kids take off their shoes and socks. Divide the class into two teams. Each team should form pairs and line up next to a water slide. **Some parts of a river are called rapids because the water moves very fast over the rocks. When people ride through the rapids on rafts, we call it "shooting the rapids!" Your partner will pull your raft through these wild river rapids, so hold on tight!**
2. Turn on the water. The first player on each team sits on an inner tube or raft while the partner walks by the water slide and pulls the raft down the slide. Partners switch places on their return trip. Then the next pair of players "shoots the rapids." Continue until everyone has had a turn. (Note: clothing will get wet! At the end of the game, have students use towels to dry off as much as possible.)

Option
For a dry version of this game, set sports cones in a grassy area to make two obstacle courses. Make "rafts" by tying ropes around inner tubes, putting them inside plastic bags and knotting bags to close around the ropes. One player from each team sits on the raft while a partner pulls the raft through the obstacle course. Partners switch places for the return trip. Younger kids may need to play this version without pulling another child in the raft. Either they may pull empty rafts through a slalom course or have an adult pull them one way and then kids pull the raft back by themselves to start.

Super Soccer

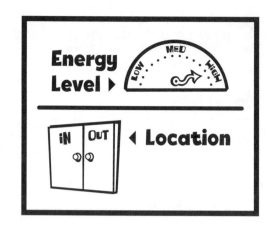

Energy Level ▶ LOW MED HIGH

◀ Location iN OuT

Materials
2 large, heavy-duty trash bags; newspaper; duct tape; masking tape, chalk, or rope

Preparation
To make a giant ball, place one trash bag inside the other. Crumple sheets of newspaper into balls to stuff into trash bags. When bags are full of newspaper balls, tie the handles into a knot and secure with a length of duct tape. Wrap the entire stuffed bag twice with duct tape, making a crisscross pattern (see sketch). Use masking tape, chalk, or rope to mark goal lines at opposite sides of the playing area, approximately 20' apart.

Lead the Game
1. **Raise your hand if you've ever been on a soccer team. Soccer is played by people all over the world; but in many countries, it's called football!** Let kids play soccer using the ball you've prepared. As in regular soccer, only the goalies can use their hands.
2. Divide the group into two teams of six to eight students. Each team chooses a goalie to stand on the far side of his or her team's goal line. Students kick the ball down the field, to another teammate, or across the goal line. A point is awarded each time the ball crosses a team's goal line.

Options
1. Backwards Ball—While playing, kids walk, run, and kick the ball backward.
2. Three-Legged Soccer—Each team divides into pairs. Using a bandana or other fabric scrap, students tie ankles together and move as a pair to play the game.
3. Fabric Fun—Each team divides into pairs. Each student in each pair holds one end of a bandana or other fabric scrap as the game is played.
4. Foosball—Kids keep one foot frozen in place at all times as they play the game. Only the goalie has free movement. You may wish to use a regular soccer ball with this option.

Game Tip
This game is great for extra-large groups!

Switch-a-Towel

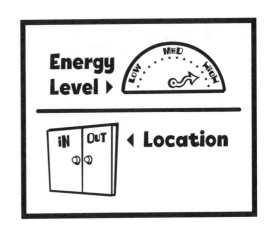

Materials
sports cones, large beach towel (for every 3 or 4 players)

Preparation
Use cones to define the boundaries of a playing area about 30' square. Spread out towels on the ground inside the playing area, leaving an open space in the middle (see sketch a).

Lead the Game
1. Select one player to be the lifeguard. The lifeguard stands in the middle of the playing area while all other players stand on the beach towels.
2. The lifeguard points to two towels and calls out, "Switch!" The players on each of those two towels try to switch places while the lifeguard tries to tag them (see sketch b). Tagged players stand outside the playing-area boundaries; in succeeding rounds they may try to tag players without re-entering the playing area. When a lifeguard calls out, "All switch!" then all players must run to another towel. Play continues until only one player remains untagged. That player becomes the lifeguard for the next game.

Option
For older kids, increase the challenge as follows: the lifeguard throws a soft, foam ball to tag players. If the ball goes out of bounds, players who have been tagged out may pick up the ball and throw it back to the lifeguard.

a.

b.

Tower Tag

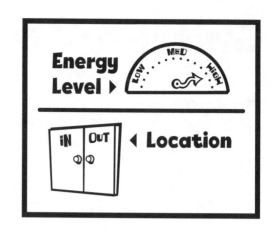
Materials
rope, cones, tape, or chalk; beanbags (or handkerchiefs); 2 baskets

Preparation
Using rope, cones, chalk, or tape, mark two team lines approximately 50' apart. Mark another line to divide that area in half. Also mark a "tower area" in opposite corners of each team's play area. Place half the beanbags or handkerchiefs on each team line. Place a basket behind each team line (see sketch). (Optional: Color-code the beanbags or use different items for each team.)

Lead the Game
1. Divide the group into two equal teams. Each team stands on their half of the playing area. At your signal, players try to grab a beanbag from the opposing team's line and return it to their own basket without being tagged. Once a player has crossed the center line with an opposing team's item, he or she is safe and cannot be tagged. If a player is tagged by an opposing team member, he or she must forfeit the beanbag and stand in the opposing team's tower. An "imprisoned" player can be released only when a fellow teammate reaches the tower without being tagged and frees him or her. Both players then receive safe passage back to their team.
2. The first team to collect all the beanbags from the other side or capture all the players on the opposite team wins.

Option
For a wet-game option, use water balloons instead of beanbags. Each team can have one or two colors of balloons for this game (team 1: yellow, red; team 2: blue, orange). For older students, tagging must be done with the water balloon (without it breaking—so no throwing).

Game Tip
This is an active game that will require refereeing.

Tower

Tower

25 feet (7.5m)

25 feet (7.5m)

Triangle Bowling

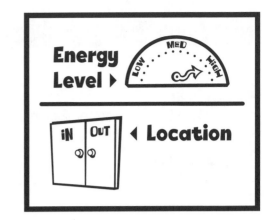
Materials

rope, chalk, or masking tape; rubber kickball

Preparation

Use rope, chalk, or tape to outline a large triangle on the ground (the bowling pin area) in the center of your playing area. Make it large enough for up to 15 students to comfortably stand inside the triangle area. Make one setup for each group of 9 to 16 students. Approximately 25' from each point of the triangle, draw or mark a foul line (see sketch).

Lead the Game

1. Choose one player as the bowler and one as the ball return. All other players are bowling pins.
2. Pins stand inside the triangle area. They choose which foot they will pivot on. The bowler stands behind the foul line and rolls the ball toward the pins, attempting to hit the players. Pins can pivot on a foot in order to avoid being hit, but they must keep one foot on the ground. The ball return stands near the pins and retrieves the ball each time, returning it to the bowler. The bowler gets two rolls. Keep track of the number of pins that the bowler hits.
3. After the bowler is finished, the bowler and ball return choose two new players and the game begins again with all other players being the pins. Continue the game until all players have had a turn at being the bowler and the ball return. Announce the top-scoring winners.

Pins

Ball Return

Option

For younger kids, shorten the distance and have them jump with both feet to avoid being hit.

Bowler

Volunteer Hoops

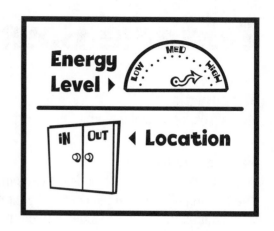

Energy Level ▶ LOW MED HIGH

Location ▶ iN OuT

Materials
index cards in 2 or more colors, 2 or more Hula-Hoops

Preparation
Mix up the index cards, and randomly scatter them in your playing area.

Lead the Game
1. Divide the group into teams of three or four. Each team is assigned one of the colors of the index cards. Give each team a Hula-Hoop. Teams spread out around the edges of your game-playing area.
2. Each team should place the hoop on the ground; then all team members are to step inside the hoop. Each team member is to hold the hoop with one hand. Teams are to quickly move through the playing area, with each student using his or her free hand to pick up the team's color of index card.
3. To determine a winner, you can set a time limit or allow all the cards to be picked up by one team. Mix up the teams and play additional rounds.

Options
1. For older students, make a rule that no hoops can touch. This will make the game slow down and focus on team strategy to collect cards. Or you could assess penalty times for hoop touching. Simply make teams freeze for ten seconds, while other teams continue to collect cards. You could also allow students to make up rules for the game.
2. Assign point values to cards, such as 100, 500, or 1,000 points. Place the cards facedown so teams won't know the value until the card is picked up. You could also make wild cards that could give the team an advantage in the game or even an instant-win card. The possibilities are endless!

Big Book of Bible Games
for Elementary Kids
© David C Cook. Permission granted to photocopy for ministry purposes only.

Water Baseball

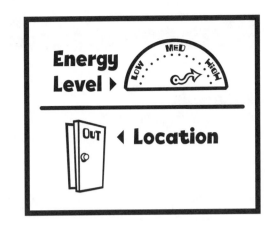

OUT ◀ Location

Materials

masking tape, chalk, or rope; tape measure; baseball tee (or sports cones); 3 sports cones; large trash can; water; baseball bat; large foam ball

Preparation

Using masking tape, chalk, or rope, mark off a diamond-shaped playing area such as used in baseball. Each side of the diamond should be approximately 20' long. Place a baseball tee or sports cone at home plate and three sports cones at the points of the diamond. Place a large trash can to the left of home plate and fill it with water.

Lead the Game

1. Divide the group into two teams. One team spreads out on the playing field with one player standing next to the trash can at home plate. The other team lines up near home plate. The first player in line stands at home plate with the baseball bat. Dunk the ball in water in the trash can until it's saturated, and then place it on the tee or sports cone.

2. On your signal, the first player hits the ball with the bat and runs around the diamond, touching the sports cones as he or she passes them. While the batter runs, the players on the other team retrieve the ball and try to get it to the player at the trash can as quickly as possible. However, the players in the field cannot run. They can only throw the ball to each other. The player at home plate dunks the ball in the water in the trash can, ending the running player's turn. (Note: If this takes awhile, the runner can run the bases two or more times.) If the ball is dropped, the nearest player runs to pick up the ball, and then returns to his or her position before throwing the ball to a teammate.

3. When the ball is in the trash can, the running player returns to home plate. His or her team is awarded one point for each sports cone that he or she touched while running. The next player in line takes a turn as described above. After three players have had a turn, teams switch positions. Continue until every student has had a turn at bat or as time permits.

Water-Well Relay

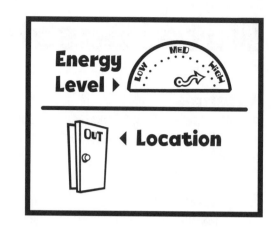

Energy Level ▶

OUT ◀ Location

Materials
wading pool (or large plastic bin), water; for each team of 6 to 8 players: large coffee can, large car-washing sponge

Preparation
Fill the wading pool or plastic bin with water. Place each team's coffee can and sponge about 20' from the wading pool or plastic bin.

Lead the Game
1. **Many people in the world don't have running water to drink. To get clean water, they go to a well each morning and gather water for that day's use. Let's play a game to carry water from the well** (indicate wading pool or plastic bin) **back to your water storage cans** (indicate coffee cans). **To give you an idea of how hard it is to gather water, we're going to use sponges to fill your cans!**
2. Divide the group into teams of six to eight players each. Teams are to line up next to their coffee cans. At your signal, the first player on each team carries the sponge to the well and gets the sponge full of water. The player runs back to the team and squeezes the water from the sponge into the coffee can, then passes the sponge to the next player in line. The game continues as time allows or until each player has had a turn. The team with the most water in its can at the end of the game wins.

Option
For older players, you can give them a variety of ways to transport the sponge (hop, run backwards, etc.).

Game Tips
1. Show younger players how to hold a sponge under water to fill it.
2. You may want to use this game to introduce a water project for a foreign mission.

Wheelbarrow Relay

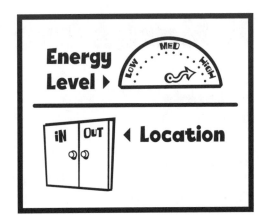

Materials
masking tape, index cards, clothespins, 2 baskets

Preparation
Use masking tape to make a starting line and finish line at least 20 feet apart on the floor. Place the baskets on the finish line.

Lead the Game
Divide the class into two teams. Each team is to line up behind the starting line next to its cards. At your signal, the first student on each team clips an index card to his or her clothing and pretends to be a "wheelbarrow" steered by the next player in line. The wheelbarrow walks on his or her hands toward the basket, while the partner steers by holding the wheelbarrow's feet (see sketch). At the basket, the wheelbarrow stands up and drops the card into the basket. He then gives the clothespin to his or her partner and runs to the back of the line. The partner returns to the front of the line and is the next wheelbarrow. The game continues in relay fashion until each student has had a chance to be a wheelbarrow.

Option
Write words of a Bible verse on the index cards. Students place the cards in order at the end of the game.

Game Tip
If you play this outside, have a pair of utility gloves for the wheelbarrows to wear, especially if playing on asphalt. Wheelbarrows should hand off gloves during the game.

X Marks the Spot

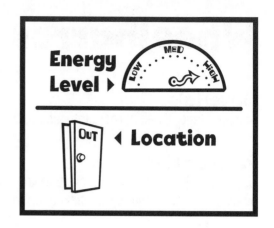

Energy Level ▶

OUT ◀ Location

Materials
chalk, several balloons

Preparation
Use chalk to draw two large circles about 15' in diameter. Make a large X in the middle of each circle. Inflate and tie the balloons.

Lead the Game
1. Divide the group into two teams. Each team is to sit inside one of the circles. Each team selects a helper who stands outside the circle. Give each of the helpers a balloon and a piece of chalk. When you say, "Launch!" each helper throws a balloon into the team's circle. The team members shout, "Warm air" and, without standing up, use their feet and hands to keep the balloon in the air. When the balloon is over the X, team members shout, "Cool air" and let it fall.
2. If the balloon touches the X, the helper gives the team a point by making a chalk mark on the pavement. If the balloon falls anywhere else, the helper retrieves the balloon and throws it into the circle again. When you say, "Stop!" the team with the most points wins.

Option
For older players, use several balloons in the circle at the same time.

15 feet (3.5 m)

Indexes

Bible Index

Energy Level Index

Low

Medium

High